Argument of L. Madison Day Before the Supreme Court United States, in the case of Commercial Bank, Manchester, vs. H.S. Buckner, on the 13th and 17th January, 1858.

Anonymous

Argument of L. Madison Day Before the Supreme Court United States, in the case of Commercial Bank, Manchester, vs. H.S. Buckner, on the 13th and 17th January, 1858.

The Making of Modern Law collection of legal archives constitutes a genuine revolution in historical legal research because it opens up a wealth of rare and previously inaccessible sources in legal, constitutional, administrative, political, cultural, intellectual, and social history. This unique collection consists of three extensive archives that provide insight into more than 300 years of American and British history. These collections include:

Legal Treatises, 1800-1926: over 20,000 legal treatises provide a comprehensive collection in legal history, business and economics, politics and government.

Trials, 1600-1926: nearly 10,000 titles reveal the drama of famous, infamous, and obscure courtroom cases in America and the British Empire across three centuries.

Primary Sources, 1620-1926: includes reports, statutes and regulations in American history, including early state codes, municipal ordinances, constitutional conventions and compilations, and law dictionaries.

These archives provide a unique research tool for tracking the development of our modern legal system and how it has affected our culture, government, business – nearly every aspect of our everyday life. For the first time, these high-quality digital scans of original works are available via print-on-demand, making them readily accessible to libraries, students, independent scholars, and readers of all ages.

old books. new life.

The BiblioLife Network

This project was made possible in part by the BiblioLife Network (BLN), a project aimed at addressing some of the huge challenges facing book preservationists around the world. The BLN includes libraries, library networks, archives, subject matter experts, online communities and library service providers. We believe every book ever published should be available as a high-quality print reproduction; printed on-demand anywhere in the world. This insures the ongoing accessibility of the content and helps generate sustainable revenue for the libraries and organizations that work to preserve these important materials.

The following book is in the "public domain" and represents an authentic reproduction of the text as printed by the original publisher. While we have attempted to accurately maintain the integrity of the original work, there are sometimes problems with the original work or the micro-film from which the books were digitized. This can result in minor errors in reproduction. Possible imperfections include missing and blurred pages, poor pictures, markings and other reproduction issues beyond our control. Because this work is culturally important, we have made it available as part of our commitment to protecting, preserving, and promoting the world's literature.

GUIDE TO FOLD-OUTS MAPS and OVERSIZED IMAGES

The book you are reading was digitized from microfilm captured over the past thirty to forty years. Years after the creation of the original microfilm, the book was converted to digital files and made available in an online database.

In an online database, page images do not need to conform to the size restrictions found in a printed book. When converting these images back into a printed bound book, the page sizes are standardized in ways that maintain the detail of the original. For large images, such as fold-out maps, the original page image is split into two or more pages

Guidelines used to determine how to split the page image follows:

• Some images are split vertically; large images require vertical and horizontal splits.
• For horizontal splits, the content is split left to right.
• For vertical splits, the content is split from top to bottom.
• For both vertical and horizontal splits, the image is processed from top left to bottom right.

ARGUMENT

OF

L. MADISON DAY

BEFORE THE

SUPREME COURT UNITED STATES,

IN THE CASE OF

COMMERCIAL BANK, MANCHESTER,

vs.

H. S BUCKNER,

ON THE 13th AND 17th JANUARY,

1858

0

May it please the Court

Your Honors will no doubt remember that memorable period in the history of our country, known as "the times of 1837."

And your Honors will also recollect the remarkable and never-to-be-forgotten influence which "those times" exerted over every pursuit in life

Under that influence, the sails of our commerce that whitened every sea were folded in repose   Our ships, which scattered the crested foam of every wave that rolled in ten thousand glittering gems over their prows, were no longer "rocked in the cradle of the deep," but slept in undisturbed and unruffled tranquility in the havens and harbors of our sea-girt shores   The monarch of the forest, that raised his high head to the clouds, ceased to bow in proud submission to the conquering power of the axe of the hardy pioneers of the West. The flood of emigration that poured over our hills, our valleys and our plains, and made the wilderness bloom and blossom like the rose in the desert, and which also, in its onward course, seemed about to o'erleap the then barrier of the Rocky Mountains, and pour down its resistless streams to where the Pacific rolls its waves of light, was checked and stayed in its onward course. The anthem of the busy hum of industry was broken, and the discordant notes were as feeble and powerless for good as the javelin thrown by the hand of old Priam to repel the invaders of that classic land.

Dark and sombre were the clouds of commercial revulsion

and disaster which overshadowed the land, and the sun of our prosperity seemed to have gone to his golden repose amid the bright beams of the beautiful West

But, happily, the night and gloom which gathered o'er the land was like that of an Arctic summer, the dawn began to re-appear before the last preceding sunset had faded from the western horizon

The genius of the nation devised, and the talent and eloquence of those whose voice, like Memnon's harp, ever rang responsive to the strains of humanity, portrayed, "in thoughts that breathe and words that burn," the necessity as well as the justness of a measure, designed to free the land from the superincumbent pressure of an untold amount of debt

Then, then it was, that that memorable and long-to-be remembered act (known as the Bankrupt Act, of 1841,) became the supreme law of the land.

The defendant in this cause, like many others, having availed himself of the provisions of that act, obtained a release and a discharge from all his debts

And the complainants, knowing of no fraud, and believing that the defendant had honestly and faithfully complied with all the requirements of the law, proved their claims and received their proportionate share of the fund surrendered

Years rolled away, and lo! the light of truth dawns upon the bankrupt and his proceedings, and the complainants start with more surprise, at the frauds disclosed, than did Beauty and Loveliness when the horrid features of the dread Mokannah, the veiled prophet of Khorassin, were unfolded to view. Finding, to their utter astonishment, that the requirements of the law had not been honestly and faithfully complied with, the bill, &c., [as on next page.]

SUPREME COURT UNITED STATES.

COMMERCIAL BANK OF MANCHESTER
vs.
HENRY S. BUCKNER.

The Bill, in this case, was filed to recover of the Defendant, a discharged bankrupt, a large sum of money, amounting in principal and interest to near One Hundred and Fifty Thousand Dollars, and contains numerous and various specifications and charges of payments, priorities, preferences, concealments and transfers of property and effects, made, done and given, (and some WITHIN SIXTY DAYS of filing the application,) in contemplation of bankruptcy, and in fraud both of the provisions and policy of the bankrupt law, as well as the just rights of creditors.

To this Bill thus charging and detailing the various and complicated frauds set forth therein, the Defendant simply filed *a naked demurrer, unaccompanied with any answer whatever denying the frauds*, or that the same had been discovered, as alleged, within the two years preceding the filing of the same.

The District Judge to whom the cause was submitted, without argument, sustained the *naked* demurrer of the Defendant, and dismissed the Bill, and to reverse this decision the Plaintiffs have appealed to this Court

With this statement of the case let us pass to the consideration of the law and the authorities applicable to the same as we doubt not but that they will show conclusively that the demurrer ought to have been overruled, and the Defendant ordered to answer the charges of fraud.

I.   The first point that naturally arises is, are the various charges of fraud (all of which are unconditionally admitted by the *naked* demurrer to be true , 11 Wheat. R. 171. 3 Pet. R 36, 6 How R 118, 2 J J Mar 405, 18 Conn R 431, 2 Gillman's R. 387), sufficient to invalidate the discharge in bankruptcy? That they are is too well settled by the highest and most respectable authorities to admit of any doubt or controversy

The second section of the bankrupt act provides .

" That all future payments, securities, conveyances or transfers of property, or agreements made or given by any bankrupt, in contemplation of bankruptcy, and for the purpose of giving any creditor, endorser, surety or other person, any preference or priority over the general creditors of such bankrupts, and all other payments, securities, conveyances or transfers of property, or agreements made or given by such bankrupt in contemplation of bankruptcy, to any person or persons whatever, not being a *bona fide* creditor or purchaser, for a valuable consideration, without notice, shall be deemed utterly void and a fraud upon this act ; and the assignee under the bankruptcy shall be entitled to claim, sue for, recover and receive the same as a part of the assets of the bankruptcy ; and the person making such unlawful preferences and payments, shall receive no discharge under the provisions of this act " 5 U S Stat 442

"It will be seen by this," (says the Court of Appeals of New York, in Caryl vs Russell 3 Kernan's R 194, 197), 'that all future payments, conveyances or transfers of property made by a bankrupt in contemplation of bankruptcy, and for the purpose of giving any person a preference or priority, are utterly void and a fraud upon the act, that the assignee may sue for and recover the same as a part of the assets, and the person guilty of these acts shall receive no discharge "

And in Buckingham, et al vs McLean, 13 How R 151, 167, Mr Justice Curtis in delivering the unanimous opinion of this Court, as to the true construction of this portion of the bankrupt law, after stating and recognizing the common law right of a debtor to prefer one *bona fide* creditor over his other creditors, well says "This common law right it was the object of the second section of the act to restrain," and then proceeded to state and hold that the giving a preference in contemplation of bankruptcy was *fraudulent* and void

Indeed it has been *held* by Mr Justice McLean on several occasions that the mere fact of a preference having been made within two months of filing the application (and the bill shows preferences and payments to a considerable amount, not only within two months but *even within a few days of the application*), was, if not in terms, impliedly fraudulent and void under the second section of the bankrupt act, which provides "that all dealings and transactions by and with any bankrupt *bona fide* made and entered into more than two months before the petition filed against him, or by him, shall not be invalidated or affected by this act."

"This," (says Judge McLean, 3 McLean's R 197) "by the strangest implication, declares that any transaction of the above nature, 'made and entered into,' *less* than two months before the petition was filed, shall be void."

So in 3 McLean's R 203, it is said . 'And the fact that the assignment was made within two months preceding the application *for relief*, is, *under the second section*, if not in terms, impliedly fraudulent '

Again, in 3 McLean's R 628-9, Mr. Justice McLean says of this provision ' Now this very clearly implies that transactions within the two months, though *bona fide*, are not valid For to make transactions valid before the two months, they must have been entered into in good faith."

And at pages 630-1 of this same authority, it is well said . " Where a suit had been commenced in the ordinary cause of judicial proceedings, and a judgment had been entered within two months it might not be void But where, by the consent of the bankrupt, the proceeding is commenced in a few days, within the two months, there could be no more glaring and indisputable act of fraud against the bankrupt law " See also 13 How R 171

In 5 Law Rep 458, Judge Irwin well says " One leading and important object of the act, is, to place the creditors of a bankrupt, upon an equality in the distribution of his assets ; and to effect this, in the first section, ' any fraudulent conveyance, assignment,' etc , is made an act of bankruptcy, and in the second section, all ' payments, securities,' etc with preferences, in contemplation of bankruptcy, are declared to be a fraud upon the act."

And Mr. Justice Thompson, in speaking of preferences,

(5 Law Rep. 312,) admirably remarks . And all such conveyances are declared to be 'utterly void, and *a fraud upon this act.*' This must refer to the acts before specified as acts of bankruptcy Why is giving a preference to be considered a fraud on this act? Because the act contemplates an equal distribution. It is a fraud because it counteracts the policy of the law. Though it may not be fraudulent in a moral point of view, it must be fraudulent if it contravenes the policy of the law " See also 3 McLean, 594

In Bell vs Leggett, 3 Seld R 179, 180, 181, the Court of Appeals of New York well says "All contracts or agreements which have for their object any thing which is repugnant to justice, or against the general policy of the common law, or contrary to the provisions of any statute are void "

" The policy of the English bankrupt act, as well as our insolvent laws and our late bankrupt act is, that a full and fair disclosure and surrender of the property of the debtor should be obtained; and that on such disclosure and surrender, he should be discharged from his debts, and his creditors be placed upon an equal footing, without preference, except where liens existed, in respect to his property, thus subjected to the control and disposition of the law. Any transaction or agreement which tends to defeat either of these objects is inconsistent with the *policy* of the law, illegal and void "

And in the case of Gassett et al. vs Morse et al , 21 Vt R 629, Mr. Justice Prentiss, in construing the bankrupt act, uses this emphatic language . " A conveyance or assignment, which is fraudulent at common law, is undoubtedly within the meaning of the act ; and so is every conveyance or assignment, which contravenes the provisions and object of the act, though good at common law The act, for instance, prohibits all preferences, and with the exception of certain specified priorities, liens and securities, declares that the property of the bankrupt shall be distributed *pro rata*, among his creditors Any conveyance or assignment, therefore, which is intended and operates to defeat this provision, though ever so fair as between the parties to it, and entirely unimpeachable on general principles of law, is a fraudulent conveyance, and consequently an act of bankruptcy " The making of payments, preferences, etc then, in contemplation of bankruptcy, must be treated and regarded as a fraud upon one of the main purposes of the law

And by the fourth section of the act it is provided. " That if any such bankrupt shall be guilty of any fraud or wilful concealment of his property, or rights of property, or shall have preferred any of his creditors contrary to the provisions of this act, or shall wilfully omit or refuse to comply with any order or directions of such Court. ~ to conform to any other requisites of this act, or shall, in the proceedings under this act, admit a false or fictitious debt against his estate, he shall not be entitled to any such discharge or certificate " 5 U S Stat 443-4

It is also further provided in this section of the act, as follows "And such discharge and certificate, when duly granted, shall in all courts of justice, be deemed a full and complete discharge of all debts, contracts, and other engagements of such bankrupt, which are proveable under this act, and shall be and may be pleaded as a full and complete bar to all suits brought in any court of judicature whatever, and the same shall be conclusive evidence of itself in favor of such bankrupt, unless the same shall be impeached for some fraud or wilful concealment by him of his property or rights of property, as aforesaid, contrary to the provisions of this act," etc 5 U S Stat. 444

From this provision of the act, it is seen, that the discharge and certificate may be impeached " for some fraud or wilful concealment by him of his property, or rights of property as aforesaid, contrary to the provisions of this act."

Every act therefore, which is a fraud on the law, (and we have seen above that the giving of preferences, etc., in contemplation of bankruptcy, has uniformly been held to be fraudulent, because it is not only contrary to the provisions and policy of the act, but is expressly declared by the same to be a *fraud on the act*) will invalidate the discharge and certificate

In Brereton vs. Hull, 1 Denio's R 75, Chief Justice Bronson, in considering this question, says · " The first question made at the bar is, whether the discharge can be impeached for the preferences among creditors, and the other payments and transfers of property, made in contemplation of bankruptcy, which are forbidden by the second section of the act I think it may. The discharge of the bankrupt may be impeached " for some fraud, or wilful concealment by him of his property, or rights of property " (§4) " Fraud is a very comprehensive term, and I cannot doubt that it includes those 'unlawful preferences,' payments and transfers of property which the statute declares 'utterly void and a fraud upon this act' (§2). It is true that the section goes on to provide, that 'the persons making such unlawful preferences and payments shall receive no discharge,' and this, it is said is the only penalty. It is of course the only penalty where a discharge is denied. But here a discharge has been granted. That does not obliterate the fraud, it still remains, and may, I think, be set up as an impeachment of the discharge. The fourth section denies a discharge to a bankrupt who shall be 'guilty of any fraud, or wilful concealment of his property,' and yet the same section provides, that the discharge may be impeached for fraud, or wilful concealment of property. This shows that the same matter—so far as relates to fraud and concealment—may be set up in answer to the discharge when granted, that might have been successfully urged against the bankrupt's application.'

And in Beekman vs Wilson, 9 Met R. 439–40, Mr. Justice Dewey in delivering the opinion of the Supreme Court of Massachusetts, in reference to the provision in the fourth section of the bankrupt act, which provides that the discharge and certificate may "be impeached for some fraud or wilful concealment by him of his property or rights of property as aforesaid, contrary to the provisions of this act," said. The position taken for the Defendant, that the fraud here referred to is fraud at the common law exclusively, is not the true construction of the statute, but, on the contrary, all those acts described in the second section, as frauds upon the bankrupt act, are embraced in the provisions of the fourth section, which declares the causes by reason of which the discharge may be avoided.

This construction seems to be entirely in accordance with the purposes of the act, and fairly within its language It is in conformity with the decision of Brereton vs Hull 1 Denio, 75, where it was held that the same matter may be set up in avoidance of the discharge, that might have been insisted upon against the application for such discharge See also Miller vs Black 1 Barr 420. These acts would, under the English decisions, be frauds upon the bankrupt system, and much more so should they be so held under ours, the second section of our statute declaring them to be 'a fraud upon the act' They are therefore, to be considered as embraced in the provisions of the fourth section, and when established by the proper proof, they are a good and sufficient answer to the certificate of discharge '

Again, in Coates vs Blush et al, 1 Cushing s R 564, the Supreme Court of Massachusetts, through Mr Justice Metcalf after quoting the principal provisions of the second and fourth sections of the act, says " In the latter of these clauses," (that is, the clause of the fourth section) " the only enumerated causes for impeaching a discharge, are fraud and wilful concealment of property by the bankrupt, though in the former clause, not only fraud and concealment of property by him, but also a preference given by him to any creditor, a wilful omission by him to comply with any orders of the Court, or to conform to any other requisitions of the act, and the admitting by him of any false or fictitious debt against his estate, are made sufficient cause for withholding a discharge And it was contended by counsel, in the case of Beekman vs Wilson, 9 Met 434, that a preference given

2

by a bankrupt to one of his creditors was not a cause for impeaching his discharge, although it might have prevented his obtaining it; and that the fraud, for which a discharge might be impeached, was fraud at the common law exclusively, and not those acts which are declared, by the second section of the bankrupt law, to be a fraud on that law But it was held otherwise, in that case, and the discharge was decided to be void, by reason of the bankrupts having preferred one creditor to another The same was held in Brereton vs Hull. 1 Denio, 75, where it was also further held that a discharge might be impeached and avoided by reason of the bankrupts having made payments and transfers of property, in contemplation of bankruptcy We are of opinion that the word 'fraud' is used in the same sense in both clauses of the fourth section, and that it means something more than the acts which are mentioned in connection with it In the latter clause, 'fraud or wilful concealment of property' are the only terms used Yet concealment is a fraud In the former clause, 'fraud' is united with all the enumerated causes for withholding a discharge, most of which, if not all, are frauds The word 'fraud' must therefore have a meaning which reaches and operates beyond all those enumerated causes. Otherwise, it is superfluous And our opinion is, that the word, in both clauses, means at least, all conduct of the bankrupt which is a fraud upon the bankrupt act, whether declared by the act to be such, or not. The purpose of the act was to discharge debtors, upon their honestly giving up their property to be equally divided among their creditors All concealment of property, all preferences of one creditor over another, and all other acts inconsistent with good faith, are to be regarded as fraudulent, and as sufficient causes for barring the debtor's claim to a discharge, and to avoid a discharge after it is granted '

In Gore vs Lawrence, 6 Fost (N H.) R 491, the Court uses this emphatic language 'Now if we can hold this conveyance to have been made in contemplation of taking the benefit of the bankrupt act, it will render void the certificate

' The provisions of the fourth section of the bankrupt act, referred to by counsel, relate to frauds and conceal-ments contrary to the provisions of the act and not to frauds generally, as stated in the argument "

And in the late case of Caryl vs Russell, 3 Kernan's R 194, the Court of Appeals of New York have given their unqualified recognition to the doctrine as laid down by Chief Justice Bronson, in Brereton vs. Hull, 1 Denio, 75, and Mr. Justice Dean in delivering the unanimous opinion of the Court (except Chippen J , who being a relative of one of the parties took no part in the decision), well and admirably says in reference to preferences, etc ·
"It is admitted on both sides that these facts, if proved on the application for a discharge, would have prevented the debtor from obtaining it It must also be conceded that any means by which a debtor in contemplation of bankruptcy, succeeds in effecting a preference among his creditors, is a fraud upon the bankrupt act, and that the whole theory of the law is equality of distribution of a bankrupt's estate

"Now such a preference, (that is ' a preference and priority given after the passage of the act in *contempla-*

tion of bankruptcy,') is declared to be a fraud upon the act, and the discharge 'may be impeached for some fraud contrary to the provisions of the act' What else is preference or priority mentioned in the replication, but a fraud contrary to the provisions of the act' Indeed, the second section makes all such preferences and priorities not only void but a fraud upon the act. How can they be declared void unless they are fraudulent , and how can such be deemed 'a fraud upon the act' without being at the same time a 'fraud contrary to the provisions of the act''"

And in reference to the case of the North American Fire Insurance Company vs Graham 5 Sand S C R 197, and the decision of the lower Court the Court of Appeals in concluding its opinion in the above case of Caryl vs Russel, holds this striking and forcible language " The error of the Superior Court and of the Supreme Court in this case is in leaving out in their interpretation a portion of the sentence which declares what may be alleged to impeach the discharge and then holding that the fraud contemplated by the act, must be some criminal act and not a legal fraud merely. I do not think the act of Congress is susceptible of any such interpretation , and am of opinion that the judgment should be reversed and a new trial ordered "

From this review of the authorities, it must be more than manifest that the giving of preferences and making conveyances and transfers of property in contemplation of bankruptcy as charged in the bill, and unqualifiedly admitted by the demurrer to be true, are such a *"fraud* as would have prevented the Defendant from obtaining

his discharge, had they been known, and that they are
also such a *"fraud"* as will invalidate the discharge after
it has been granted

II.   The equity side of the Circuit Court has jurisdiction
of the cause

That the bank had the right to institute suit in the Cir-
cuit Court we think there can be no doubt.   It is alleged
in the bill that the bank is a corporation by the laws of
Mississippi, and located in said State, and that the Defendant is a citizen of Louisiana, residing in the Eastern
District of the same   This is all that was necessary to
give jurisdiction, as it is now the settled doctrine of this
Court, that a corporation may sue in the Circuit Court
Marshall vs Baltimore and Ohio Railroad Company, 16
How R. 314 , Louisville Railroad Company vs. Letson,
2 How R. 497

And we think it is equally well settled by this Court,
that the *equity side* of the Circuit Court has jurisdiction of
the cause

For the equity jurisdiction of the Federal Courts is the
same in nature and extent in all the States, and is entirely
independent of the local law of any State, and is the same
in nature and extent as the equity jurisdiction of England,
from which it is derived, and it is no objection to this
jurisdiction that there is a remedy under the local law

In Boyce's Exs. vs Grundy, 3 Pet 215, Mr. Justice
Johnson, in delivering the opinion of the Court, says
"this Court has been often called upon to consider the
sixteenth section of the Judiciary Act of 1789, and as
often, either expressly or by the course of its decisions,

has held, that it is merely declaratory, making no alteration whatever in the rules of equity on the subject of legal remedy. See also Bean vs Smith, 2 Mason 252.

So Mr Justice Washington. in Harrison vs Rowan, 4 Wash C C. 205 *held* that the 16th section of the act of 1789, did not abridge or restrict the equity jurisdiction, and that it went no farther than to recognize and adopt the long and well established principles of the English Court of Chancery, upon the subject of the ordinary jurisdiction of a Court of Equity, and said, "Any other construction would unsettle those great land marks which have hitherto separated the two jurisdictions of Common Law and Equity Courts, and would introduce all that uncertainty which is usually attended upon every new system."

And in 6 Ohio R 429-30, and 9 Mo R. 339, a similar construction has been put upon State laws, substantially the same as the 16th section of the judiciary act

In the case of the United States vs Myers et al, 2 Brock R 525, Mr. Justice Thompson after stating that it had been decided "again and again," that the provision of the sixteenth section of the judiciary act, was nothing but an affirmation of the well known principle in equity, that a party cannot come into equity when he has a plain, adequate and complete remedy at law, says — "The principle which we are now considering, applies to those cases in which ordinarily, the only remedy is at law, but the party comes into equity on the ground, that by reason of some impediment in the way, or some unfair legal advantage acquired by his adversary, justice cannot be done him at law. The Court inquires whether such impediment or legal advantage exists, and accordingly, as

it *does*, or *does not*, grants, or withholds relief But it
does not apply to those cases, in which the courts of equity and law, have a concurrent jurisdiction In those
cases, although the concurrent jurisdiction of the court of
equity most probably originated, from the consideration
that there *was not* or *might not be*, an adequate remedy at
law, yet where that concurrent jurisdiction has been
established, if a party elect to come into a court of equity,
it is no objection to its jurisdiction in the given case, that
the party might have remedy at law, even although, in
that particular case, the remedy might be adequate "

For, as is well said by Mr Justice Call in 5 Leigh's R
55 'It will be observed that the very phrase (concurrent
jurisdiction,) gives the idea that equity may act where
there is also a remedy at law, and the cases show this
clearly. '

So in Mayer vs. Foulkrod, 4 Wash. C. C 354–6, Mr
Justice Washington after stating that the Plaintiff could,
perhaps have as complete a remedy in a Court of law of
the State, as it were possible for such a Court to give,
says ' The conclusive answer is, that the Plaintiff is under no obligation to resort to that jurisdiction,' and then
proceeds to illustrate and assert the doctrine that the
equity side of the Federal Courts would still retain jurisdiction, ' if such jurisdiction could be asserted as belong-
ing to that side of the Court,' notwithstanding the party
by the local law might have an adequate remedy on the
law side of the Court

And the uniform course of decision in this Court has
been that the Federal Courts in exercising chancery jurisdiction, are in no way or manner whatever influenced or

controlled by the jurisdiction and practice of the State
Courts ; but that they proceed in equity causes according
to the principles, rules and usages which belong to Courts
of Equity as contra-distinguished from Courts of Common
Law , that the acts of Congress have distinguished between
remedies at common law and equity, and that to effectuate
the purposes of the legislature, the remedies in the Courts
of the United States are to be at common law or in equity,
not according to the practice of the State Courts, but according to the principles of common law and equity as
distinguished and defined in that country from which we
derive our knowledge of those principles, and that consequently when relief can be given by the English chancery,
similar relief may be given by the Courts of the Union,
and that it is no objection to this jurisdiction that there is
a remedy under the local law.

Robinson vs Campbell, 3 Wheat R. 212; Gaines vs
Relf et al , 15 Pet 14–15; Neves et al. vs. Scott et al ,
13 How R. 272; United States vs. Howland, 4 Wheat R
115, Boyle vs. Zacharie et al , 6 Pet. R 658, Livingston
vs Story, 9 Pet 654, State Penn vs. Wheeling B. Co. et
al , 13 How R 563–4

And in Dodge vs. Woolsey, 18 How. 347, Mr Justice
Wayne, in an elaborate opinion, says "That this Court
and other Courts of the United States had repeatedly
decided that the equity jurisdiction of the Courts of
the United States is independent of the local law of any
State, and is the same in nature and extent as the equity
jurisdiction of England, from which it is derived, and that
it is no objection to this jurisdiction, that there is a remedy under the local law. Gordon vs Hobart. 2 Sumner,
C. C. Rep. 401."

Having thus conclusively established by the repeated decisions of this Court, that the jurisdiction of the equity side of the Circuit Court in Louisiana, is the same as that of similar Courts in other States, and is co-extensive with the equity jurisdiction of the English Chancery as defined in England, (and we may add those States of the Union that have recognized and adopted the same,) our next and only inquiry, in order to completely establish and settle the question of jurisdiction, is to ascertain whether the case made by the bill is of such a nature and character as to give equity jurisdiction?

We unhesitatingly claim that it is, and have the utmost confidence that we shall be fully borne out both by the *English* and *American* authorities

The great and leading question, as made by the bill. is one of fraud Fraud lies at the foundation, and it is on this ground that we claim relief in equity.

All the frauds charged in the bill being *admitted* by the *naked* demurrer, we present a case, which, beyond all doubt, entitles us to invoke the aid of Chancery, even if we had a remedy at law. For in all cases of fraud, excepting fraud in obtaining a will, equity has a concurrent jurisdiction with a Court of law.

This doctrine as early as the year 1714, was clearly recognized and laid down by the highest Court of England (the House of Lords) in the case of Booth vs. Lord Warrington, 1 Brown's Parl. Ca. 445, 4 ib. 163, (Tomlin's ed) and has ever since, down to the present time, been steadily and uniformly adhered to, not only in England, but in the most respectable Courts throughout the country.

That was a case in which the Plaintiff, by the false and

fraudulent representations of the Defendant, had been induced to believe, and to pay a large sum of money to the Defendant, on the ground that he, the Defendant, had paid, or was bound to pay said sum for having procured the Plaintiff's marriage with a lady of fortune Nine years after that, the Plaintiff discovered the fraud, and ascertained the fact that the Defendant had neither paid, nor was bound to pay, anything whatever on account of said marriage He then filed his bill to recover back the money thus fraudulently obtained, and on a full hearing before the House of Lords, the jurisdiction was maintained, notwithstanding, as was held, an action at law might have been maintained to recover damages for the fraud, and this ruling of that high tribunal has been adopted and acted upon both by jurists and the most learned of courts.

So again, in the year 1723, in the case of Colt vs Woollaston, 2 P. Wms 154, 156, which was a bill filed to recover back money which Plaintiff had been fraudulently induced by Defendant to pay for stock in a company on the representation that it was of great value and no risk, but which, in fact, was but a bubble, it was *held* that *equity had jurisdiction* notwithstanding there was a clear remedy at law

At page 156 of this authority, the Master of the Rolls well says : " If this were a fraud against any private or single person, a Court of Equity would relieve , *a fortiori* where it is a fraud against great numbers, against multitudes, where the mischief is more extensive, and many families thereby ruined

" It is no objection that the parties have their remedy

at law, and may bring an action for moneys had and received for the Plaintiffs' own use, for in a case of fraud
the Court of Equity has a concurrent jurisdiction with the
common law, matter of fraud being the great subject of
relief here "

In Blair vs Bromley, 5 Hare R 542, 26 Eng, Ch R.
541, where one of two partners at law had committed a
fraud by misapplying certain moneys received for invest-
ment and continued falsely to represent that they were
properly invested, but of all which the other partner had
no knowledge whatever, it was *held* that the latter
was nevertheless liable for the fraud of his partner
after the dissolution of the firm, and that equity had jurisdiction on the ground of fraud, notwithstanding an action
might lie at law

Mr Vice Chancellor Wigram, in the above case, 26
Eng. Ch. 555-6, says · Then the only question is, whether the relief is in equity or at law. Supposing it to be
prima facie a case cognizable in a court of law, and not a
case for equity, the Plaintiffs must get over that difficulty
by showing that the case is, on some ground, brought
within the jurisdiction of this Court, as that which is here
relied on, namely, fraud or misrepresentation." And
after stating that if the bill had been filed against the partner who had committed the fraud, he had not, " for a
moment entertained a doubt" but that " he might have
been charged in this Court," because he would have imputed to him the continued misrepresentation made at the
beginning down to the discovery of the fraud, this same
learned Vice Chancellor says · " There would be both
suppressio veri and *suggestio falsi ;* and the case would fall

within the common principle of the jurisdiction of the Court ," and concludes his opinion as follows · " The jurisdiction of this Court is assumed on the ground of fraud."

So in Brydges vs Bramliff, 12 Simons, 369, 35 Eng. Ch. 313, relief was given in equity against two innocent partners in a case very similar in principle to the case of Blair vs Bromley, and at page 331 of this case, (35 Eng Ch ,) the Court says: " The substantial ground for relief is the fraud in the excessive price "

So in Wilson vs Short, 6 Hare R., 31 Eng. Ch. 366, it is held that there is a remedy in equity as well as at law, by a principal against his broker or agent to recover back a sum of money paid to the broker on his *untrue* representation that he had entered into a contract for his principal, which alleged contract had, in fact, no existence. In this case, the learned Vice Chancellor, at pages 383, 384, says " The original jurisdiction to try a right depending upon such considerations is not ousted because the right might be tried at law."

"And the suit, as I before observed, is sustainable upon the distinctive ground of misrepresentation, which, whatever its moral character may be, this Court deals with as fraud."

Mr. Daniell (2 Danl. Ch. P. 611) says "Amongst other cases in which Courts of equity and Courts of law entertain a concurrent jurisdiction, are those arising upon frauds; therefore where fraud is made the ground for the interference of this Court, a demurrer will not hold."

And on the appeal of the above cited case of Blair vs. Bromley, in 1847, 2 Philips, Ch. R. 354; 22 Eng. Chan.

R. 353, to the High Court of Chancery in England, the decision of Vice Chancellor Wigram was affirmed

The Lord Chancellor Cottenham, in concluding his judgment in this case, says 'What I have already said, and the cases to which I have referred, make it unnecessary to say much upon the objection that the Plaintiff's remedy, if any, is at law." "In all these cases, the effect of the misrepresentation raises an equity to restore the parties deceived as nearly as possible to the situation in which, but for the misrepresentation, they would have stood, and for which damages in an action might be a very inadequate remedy, and it is no objection to this equity. that the facts may also support an action " 'It is more than one hundred and twenty years since a similar objection was made, in Colt vs Woollaston, and overruled. I am, therefore, of opinion that the decree of the Vice Chancellor Wigram must be affirmed, with costs '

And in Ranger vs. The Great Western Railway Co , 27 Eng. L and Eq. R. 35, the House of Lords has given its unqualified recognition to the doctrine, that in cases of fraud and account, equity has jurisdiction of a purely legal right, even if the party has a remedy at law

Lord Chancellor Cottenham, in his opinion in this case, (page 42) says "Is it established that any imposition was practised on the appellant to induce him to enter into the contract? For if there was, he was clearly entitled to relief." And after examining the evidence, and concluding the charges of fraud were not made out, he continues "This, therefore, brings us to the question whether, independently of these two heads of fraud, the Appellant has shown a title to relief." "His object is to obtain payment for work done by him for the Company under several contracts, to which I have referred. Now, *prima facie,* the payment ought to be sought, not through the medium of a suit in equity, but by an action at law The right of the Appellant is strictly a legal right—the obligation of the Company is a mere legal obligation " And then his Lordship proceeded to state and *hold* that the jurisdiction was sustainable, notwithstanding the failure to prove the fraud, as an account was necessary

Now, the above case in the House of Lords in 1854, is doubly important as it not only clearly recognizes and maintains the doctrine, that equity in cases of *fraud* has jurisdiction of a strictly legal right, but also holds that, though the fraud may not be proved, and consequently relief cannot be given on that ground, yet the bill may be maintained for an account, and thereby the party obtain relief in equity This case, then, fully sustains the jurisdiction in the case before the Court, both on the ground of fraud and account, for not only is the fraud established, by. the admission of the demurrer, but the bill shows the necessity, and prays for an account. And to this might be added the following, with many other authorities, that law and equity have concurrent jurisdiction in matters of account 4 Dess 474, 1 Term Rep 487 ; 2 Litt. 72 , 4 Monroe 581 ; 10 Yerg 121 , 2 Stew. R 420; 1 Ves. 173, 20 J R 584

Having thus shown by the English cases that from the year 1714 to 1854, the British Courts and the House of Lords have uniformly and steadily affirmed the doctrine that in cases of *fraud*, equity has jurisdiction even if there be a remedy at law, we might well conclude this branch of the case , but as the same doctrine has been frequently and repeatedly recognized on this side of the Atlantic, it may not be unimportant to refer to some of the most prominent American authorities

In Phalen vs Clark, 19 Conn. R 421, the Supreme Court of Errors of Connecticut, in an elaborate and well considered opinion, *held*, that a Court of Equity has jurisdiction to relieve against every species of *fraud*, and in many cases concurrently with a court of law

At pages 433-4 of this authority, the Court says " A further objection to this proceeding, is, that the remedy at law is adequate by an action of *indebitatus assumpsit*

"There is no doubt but such an action could have been sustained, in a case like this, but from this it cannot be assumed that a Court of Law would have exclusive jurisdiction. Fraud, here, lies at the foundation; it is the ground of complaint, and the Plaintiffs seek relief from its effects. Lord Hardwick has said, that a Court of Equity has undoubted jurisdiction to relieve against every species of fraud Chancellor Kent, too, lays it down as a principle, that fraud and damage, coupled together, will entitle the injured party to relief in any Court of justice The leading case of Booth vs. Lord Warrington 4 Brown's Parl Cas 163, (Toml ed.) in this cannot well be distinguished from the present. Evans vs Bucknell, 6 Ves. 174, Bacon vs Bronson. 7 Johns. Ch. R. 194, 1 Sto. Eq. 195"

And in Hagan vs. Walker et al, 14 How 29, this Court held that a Court of Equity has jurisdiction of a bill against the administrator of a deceased debtor, and a person to whom real and personal property was conveyed by the deceased debtor for the purpose of defrauding creditors, and that the Court in such a case does not exercise an auxiliary jurisdiction to aid legal process, "but comes under a head of original jurisdiction in equity," (ib. 33 Per Mr Justice Curtis,) and consequently it is not necessary that the creditor should be in a situation to levy execution if the fraudulent obstacle should be removed

"Fraud," says the Court in Kentucky, in 5 B. Mon R 598, "presents peculiar claims to the interposition of the Chancellor."

In Briggs vs French, 1 Sum. R 504, Judge Story in answer to the objection of a want of jurisdiction said : "But a Court of Equity has a clear concurrent jurisdiction with Courts of Law in cases of fraud"

And in Massie vs Watts, 6 Cranch 158, Chief Justice Marshall says "This Court is of opinion that in cases of fraud, of trust or of contract, the jurisdiction of a Court of Equity is sustainable wherever the person be found."

In Gaines vs. Chew, 2 How S C R 645, Mr. Justice McLean, in delivering the opinion of the Court, held, that, "In cases of fraud, equity has a concurrent jurisdiction with a Court of Law"

And in Sheppard et al, vs Iverson, 12 Alab (N.S) R. 99, Mr Justice Goldthwaite, says "At first we were inclined to think that under the case made by the bill, the complainant had an adequate remedy at law, by garnishee process, but further reflection has convinced us, that even if this remedy could be effectively pursued, it does not follow he may not also proceed in equity to set aside the fraudulent assignment, and thus reach assets which in reality belong to his debtor. Fraud is one of the original grounds upon which Courts of Equity have always considered themselves as entitled to entertain jurisdiction Daniel's Ch Prac. 611, Story's Eq , § 184 We conclude, therefore, that it is no objection to this bill, that the party might have redressed himself by pursuing his legal remedy "

So in Robinson vs Chesseldine, 4 Scam, R 332-3, it was held that equity has a concurrent jurisdiction with a Court of Law, in cases of fraud, accident and mistake, even if there be a full and ample remedy at law See 2 Bibb 583· 1 Littel, 88

Judge Story, 2 Eq Jurisp sect 68, 5th ed , says. "And cases of fraud are least of all those, in which the complete exercise of the jurisdiction of a Court of Equity in granting relief ought to be questioned or controlled; since in addition to all other reasons, fraud constitutes the most ancient foundation of its power "

And in sections 64 1 and 80, this same learned jurist says it is no objection to the jurisdiction in equity, that the Courts of Law have assumed or have had jurisdiction conferred on them by statute of a matter, of which equity formerly had jurisdiction In that case the jurisdiction would be concurrent. See also 4 Cow R 717, 727-8, 2 Bibbs R 273, 9 Mo. R 339, 6 Ohio R 429-30, 4 Monroe's R 104

Nor does the fact that the fraud, from which relief is sought, is fraud in obtaining a judgment, or discharge in bankruptcy, at all militate against or oust the Chancellor of jurisdiction

For ever since the celebrated dispute which arose in the year 1616, between the Courts of Law and Equity as to the right and authority of the latter to relieve against a judgment obtained by fraud and imposition, was determined in favor of the latter, the jurisdiction and authority of a Court of Chancery to relieve against a judgment obtained by fraud has been universally recognized and acquiesced in   3 Bl Com 54

Indeed, there is one unbroken current of authority in support of the position, that a Court of Equity will interfere and relieve a party from the operation and effect of a judgment, when there is *any* fact which shows it to be against justice or good conscience, to allow the party to avail himself of the same   2 Green's (N J) Ch R 520, 523, and numerous English authorities there cited, 1 J Ch. 402, 3 J Ch 280, 6 J, Ch 235, 2 Hen and Munf 139 2 Munf 253, 8 Geo R 306 19 Ohio R 448, 2 J J Mar 405, 12 B Mon 427, 2 Cow R 193, Bowen vs Evans, 2 House of Lords' Ca 257. 20 Conn R 544, 2 P Wm 424, 7 Cranch R 336, 2 Kernan's R 165, 3 P Wm 395, 2 Ves Jun 135, 1 Sch & Lef 205–6, 3 Dess R 323–4, 3 J. Ch. 351 Mitf Eq P. 239-44

In Van Meter vs Jones, 2 Green's (N J) R. 520, Chancellor Vroom in an elaborate and well considered opinion, after citing numerous authorities sustaining the right and jurisdiction of Chancery to relieve against fraud in judgments decrees, verdicts, awards, etc , and after further stating that it made no difference as to the jurisdiction of Chancery, if there was a concurrent jurisdiction at law, says "It" (Chancery) "exercises the power of setting aside decrees for fraud, not on the ground of concurrent jurisdiction, but by reason of an ancient, or rather an inherent authority growing out of the very principles and constitution of the Court, and extending itself over the judgments of Courts of every description "

Mr Justice Daniel, too, in Byers vs Surget, 19 How 308, in speaking on the subject of fraudulent judgments, well says ' But with any fraudulent conduct of parties in obtaining a judgment or in attempting to avail themselves thereof, this Court can regularly, as could the Circuit Court take cognizance Such a proceeding is within the legitimate province of Courts of Equity and constitutes an extensive ground of their jurisdiction The true and intrinsic character of proceedings as well in Courts of Law as *in pais*, is alike subject to the scrutiny of a Court of Equity which will probe, and either sustain or annul them, according to their real character and as the ends of justice may require '

True, a Court of Equity does not presume to direct or control a Court of Law, but, it considers all the equities between the parties and acts upon the person of the party, seeking against *good conscience* to avail himself of an advantage, which under all the equitable circumstances of the case, it is against conscience for him so to do, and restrains or deprives him of such advantage 20 Conn R 556, 2 St Eq Sects 875, 194 1 Atk 630 1 Sch & Lef. 205–6, 2 P Wm 424, 2 Ves Jun 135, 3 P W. 395

And so, even at law, (notwithstanding the general rule that no Court except an appellate one has authority or power to set aside the judgment of another Court of competent jurisdiction for error or irregularity) where the main object, as in this case, is not to annul the judgment of another Court, but simply to avoid the effect of such judgment, when it is set up as a bar, by replying that it was obtained by fraud, the party has a right to show, in any Court, that the judgment was obtained by fraud and imposition, and thus indirectly to treat it as a nullity. 2 La. R 139–40, 11 ib. 521, 25 Vt R 339; 2 Kernan's R 165 and auth. cited, 3 Cranch's R. 300, 307–8, 310–11, 3 Foster's (N H) R. 535, 3 Sum 604, Shedden vs. Patrick, 28 Eng L & Eq R 56, and the numerous cases cited by counsel on page 60, 72 Eng C L 513, 15 J R 121; 6 Pet 729–30, Don vs Lipman, 5 Clark & Finn R 1, 20, 21, St Conf. L sect 603

For if such be not the law, then a party would be allowed to profit by his own fraud, "a position altogether inadmissible " Per Thompson Ch. J. in Borden vs. Fitch, 15 J R 121

But, be this as it may on general principles, yet according to the express provisions of the bankrupt act, it is competent for any Court to treat the discharge and certificate, when interposed as a barrier to prevent a recovery on a pre-existing demand, as *null* and *void*, whenever the fraud is shown 5 U. S Stat 443-4, 8 Iredell (N. C) R. 142; Mabry et al vs. Herndon, 8 Alab R 848, 864, 11 Humphrey's R 289, 3 Dess R. 269-70, 3 Cranch R. 300, 307; 9 Geo. R. 9, 14-5, 15 Alab. R 553-4, 2 Zabrisk. R 541 , 25 Vt R 339. See also Robt Fraud. Conv. 520; 1 Dall 380, 1 Binney R. 263, 3 Har and J. 13, 6 ib 82, 5 Binn R 247.

Fraud vitiates everything into which it enters. It is like the deadly and noxious simoom of arid and desert climes. It prostrates all before its contaminating touch, and leaves death only and destruction in its train No act, however solemn, no agreement, however sacred, can resist its all-destroying power

All acts into which fraud enters are nullities

Neither a bona fide debt, nor an actual advance of money will sustain a security infected with fraud Per Sandford, Chancellor 2 Sandf Ch R 631

In the case of Downer vs Rowell, 25 Vt R 339, the Supreme Court of Vermont in construing the bankrupt act, says "The statute in effect declares that in case the discharge and certificate *were super induced* by fraud, they may be impeached on that ground, as being null and void "

And if a judgment is null and void, it is the same thing as though it had never been rendered, and is " unavailable for any purpose," (Per Thompson Ch. J , in Borden vs Fitch, 15 J R. 140; 11 S and Mar R 464, 11 La R 533, 11 Eng. Ch R 448-9), and may be *collaterally* disallowed and disregarded Slocum vs Wheeler, 1 Day's (Conn) R. 429, 449, 6 How (Miss) R 285 8 Smedes & Mar. R 519

Such being the law, then, there can be no ground for saying that the discharge and certificate should have been annulled by a direct action, instituted for that purpose, in the Bankrupt Court 2 Kernan's R 166· 8 Alab R 855-864

Indeed it has been held by high authority that the District Court never had any jurisdiction to entertain such a proceeding Mabry et al vs Herndon, 8 Alab R. 855

But if it could be shown or was conceded that the bankrupt act gave such jurisdiction to that Court, yet as the act has been unconditionally repealed, with no saving clause in the repealing act, except for the purpose of finally completing and determining causes *then* pending, the District Court is clearly without any jurisdiction for such a purpose 4 Seld R 265 For the law is well settled, that whenever a statute from which a Court derives its jurisdiction is repealed, the jurisdiction of the Court is gone, even as to suits then pending, except so far as it is expressly saved by the repealing act and that the original act conferring jurisdiction is to be regarded as though it had never existed Dwarris on Stat 676, Miller's Case 1 Wm Black R 451 4 Yeates R 394, 5 Cranch 281, 11 Pick. 350, 21 Pick. 373. 1 Hill 324, 5 Blackford's R 195. 15 Conn R. 242, 4 Humph R 427 4 Selden's R 265-9

No action of nullity, then was or could by any possibility be necessary to entitle the Complainants to recover, either at law or in equity, on their original demands

Nor was it at all necessary to apply to the District Court, for leave to impeach the discharge and certificate Chief Justice Ruffin in 8 Iredell's R 142, says it is the duty of the Court " to hold a discharge obtained by fraud as ineffectual and void, whenever the fraud shall appear The remedy of the creditor is not an application to the Court of Bankruptcy upon the ground of fraud newly discovered, but by replying the fraud of the bankrupt to the plea of discharge, so as thereby to avoid the bar " And the same doctrine is laid down by the Supreme Court of Alabama in 8 Alab R 864

In Sims vs. Slocum 3 Cranch, 300, 307 Chief Justice Marshall says " When the person who has committed the fraud attempts to avail himself of the act, so as to discharge himself from a previously existing obligation, or to acquire a benefit, the judgment thus obtained is declared void as to that purpose

And in Mabry et al vs Herndon, 8 Alabama Reports, 856-7, Chief Justice Collier, also, in an elaborate opinion, said "Thus we see that although the statute contemplated a boon to the debtor, viz a release from indebtedness, it exacted, on his part, perfect integrity, in yielding up everything that was liable to his debts If this was not done but something was wilfully withheld, to which the creditors were entitled the fact of concealment is denounced as a fraud, and upon its being made known, the Court was required to refuse its sanction to the bankrupt's discharge And if the proceedings are formally consummated by a final decree, and a certificate consequent thereupon, it is competent for any court of judicature, upon the fraud being established, to treat the certificate as a nullity See also Mitf Eq Pl 239

The Supreme Court of Tennessee, in the case of Gupton vs Connor, 11 Humph R 289, well says "If the fraud appear pending his suit against his creditors, no decree of discharge could be made If it appear afterwards, its effect is to annul and destroy the discharge and certificate, as though they had never been obtained "

And in Cogburn & Powell vs. Spence & Elliott, 15 Ala. R 553-4, the Supreme Court of Alabama very truly remarks "The bankrupt act does not intend, nor in any manner undertake to restrain a creditor who has a cause of action against a bankrupt, from sueing him, although the bankrupt may have obtained his final certificate of discharge. It only gives the bankrupt a complete defence against the cause of action, when sued That the whole scope of the act was, to furnish the bankrupt with a complete defence to suits brought against him, is still more apparent from the fact that the certificate is not a bar, if the debt is of a fiduciary character, or if the discharge be obtained *by fraud* The act, therefore only intends to arm the bankrupt with a perfect defence against all debts discharged by the certificate obtained in pursuance of the act. The creditor may, however sue on his demand; otherwise he could not dispute the *bona fides* of the certificate, and the bankrupt must rely on his certificate in bar of the suit."

Chancellor Desaussure, too, in Lowe vs Blake, 3 Dess 269, 270. in relation to an insolvent discharge, uses this strong and forcible language· "That in case there was any fraud or concealment in obtaining this discharge, this Court is not bound to give effect to the discharge obtained in any other Court That it is essential to the jurisdiction of this Court to detect fraud, and to prevent its having its intended effect, and even formal judgments at law cannot resist its all-searching power, and when the frauds on which they have been obtained are exposed, such judgments are decreed to be nullities If the discharge was obtained by fraud or concealment, it was a mere nullity, like every other judgment or sentence of a Court obtained by fraud or surreptitiously"

So in Card vs. Walbridge and others, 18 Ohio 411, 423 which is a case *directly* in point, it being a bill to subject certain property to the payment of certain debts, and to have the *certificate of bankruptcy* declared void as having been obtained in fraud of the law, the Court in sustaining the jurisdictions says

"The great question in the case is one of fraud, which has to be established before the complainant can proceed one step in his cause, and comes within the *original* powers of a Court of Chancery."

"The appropriate remedy.' (says Chancellor Walworth, Alcott vs Avery, 1 Barb Ch R 347 352,) "of the Complainant in this Court, where he wishes to contest the validity of the Defendant's discharge, subsequent to the decree. and to obtain satisfaction of the decree out of subsequently acquired property. is to file a supplemental bill. stating the obtaining of the decree, the alleged or pretended discharge of the Defendant, under the bankrupt act, subsequent to such decree, and the fraud of the Defendant which renders the alleged discharge invalid, and praying that the decree may be carried into full effect against the Defendant and his property notwithstanding his pretended discharge ' See also 9 Geo R 9–14

The pretended discharge in bankruptcy and the length of time may be urged against a recovery of the original debt—may be insisted upon to defeat the original existing right of action—and hence, the statement of those facts in the bill which show that they constitute no valid defense to the Complainant's right of recovery This is the correct mode of pleading in Chancery in which, as there is no replication the Plaintiff sets forth in his bill the pretended defenses which may be urged. and then shows the reasons why those defenses should not be sustained Hence are set forth the frauds in obtaining the discharge in bankruptcy, and the concealment of the fraud, for the purpose of avoiding the defense of the discharge in bankruptcy if it should be plead, (as it must be, 5 U S Stat 444, Mif Eq Pl 241, 17 Alab. 554,) and also as giving a reason why the statute of limitations does not apply. Story's Eq. Pl sect. 31, and sects. 677, 678.

"It is unquestionable," says the Court of Appeals of New York in Dodson vs Pearce, 2 Kernan's R. 165, "that a Court of Chancery has power to grant relief against judgments when obtained by fraud '

So in Davis vs Tileston et al , 6 How 114, 120, this Court said "The demurrer admits the fraud thus set out, and the law is undoubted that our jurisdiction in equity extends over frauds generally "

And again in Shelton vs Tiffin et al., 6 How 163, 185, it is *held* that where *fraud* is alleged in a bill, and relief prayed against a judgment and judicial sale of property a demurrer to the same on the ground that relief can be be had at law *cannot* be sustained

The jurisdiction of equity, therefore, is clearly maintainable on the distinctive ground of fraud in obtaining the discharge in bankruptcy And besides where the remedy in equity is less difficult and more full and complete than at law, equity has jurisdiction of the cause Wylie vs Coxe, 15 How 420. Hogan vs Walker et al 14 How 29, Taylor vs Mers T Ins Co , 9 How. 405.

Now in cases of fraud, the remedy in equity is more full and complete and less difficult than at law, and this is a sufficient authority for the interposition of the Chancellor.

In Harrison vs Rowan, 4 Wash C. C 205, Mr Justice Washington well and admirably says "Proceeding, then, upon the ground of the established jurisdiction of the Court of Chancery, we know that there are a number of cases in which a concurrent jurisdiction is exercised by the two Courts, and in many of them, the ground of the equity jurisdiction is *not* that the common law courts are incompetent to afford a remedy, but that such a *remedy is less complete* than the Court of Equity, from the nature of its organization, is capable

"Cases for example, of fraud, account, dower and partition, are clearly cognizable in the common law courts, and yet the Court of Chancery has always exercised a concurrent jurisdiction over them upon the ground above mentioned."

"We hold it therefore, to be perfectly clear, that where a case is otherwise proper for the jurisdiction of a Court of Equity, it is no objection to its exercise that the party may have a remedy at law See also 1 Wheat. 179

So Chief Justice Parker in Farnum vs Brooks, 9 Pick 224, says . ' In equity, fraud may be presumed from circumstances which might not amount to proof in a Court of Law '

And that great jurist Judge Story (whose learning and wisdom embodied in his works will live till time shall be no more,) has well and truly said That Courts of Equity do not restrict themselves by the same rigid rules as Courts of Law in the investigation of fraud, and in the evidence and proofs required to establish it It is equally a rule in Courts of Law and Courts of Equity that fraud is not to be presumed, but must be established by proofs ' And after stating that neither of said Courts ' insists upon positive and express proofs of fraud, but each deduces them from circumstances affording strong presumptions," this same distinguished author, jurist and judge, says "But Courts of Equity will act upon circumstances, as presumptions of fraud, where Courts of Law would not deem them satisfactory proofs In other words Courts of Equity will grant relief upon the ground of **fraud**, established by presumptive evidence, which evidence, Courts of Law would not always deem sufficient to justify a verdict." 1 St Eq. Sect 190, 5th ed

In equity, too, the Complainant may require the Defendant to answer all the allegations of fraud under oath without being concluded or bound as at law, by the same And, as Lord Hardwick (1 Atk 628) says "The admission of a fact by a party concerned, and who is most likely to know it, is stronger than if determined by a jury, and facts are as properly concluded by an admission, as by a trial'

Judge Story, too, has well said that "Equity sifts the conscience of the party, not only by requiring his own answer under oath, but by subjecting it to the severe scrutiny of comparison with other competent testimony; thus narrowing the chances of successful evasion, and compelling the party to do equity, as it shall appear upon a full survey of the whole transaction ' 1 St Eq , sect 68 "Courts of Equity, therefore, will exercise a concurrent jurisdiction with Courts of Law in *all* matters of fraud, excepting only of fraud in obtaining a will' 1 St Eq , sects 440, 184 See also 1 Danl. Ch P 611

Again there is a marked and manifest distinction between the rule in equity and at law, as to the burthen of proof in relation to the time of the discovery of the fraud

Now, according to the practice and law in the Courts of Louisiana, (and this would be the rule on the law side of the Circuit Court of the United States) a party who alleges fraud and the *discovery* of the same within such time as an action would lie, must not only prove the fraud, but he must go farther and prove that he discovered the same within the time alleged See 7 Rob R 92

Such being the law in Louisiana, the remedy at law would be much more difficult than in equity, the party being required at law to prove a negative

But the established and well recognized rule (in cases of fraud) in equity, is, that where fraud is alleged, and the bill charges that the fraud was discovered within such a period of time as an action will lie, it is only incumbent on the complainant to prove the fraud When he has done this he has proved enough, and it then devolves on the Defendant if he would avail himself of the bar of the statute to prove that the complainant knew of, or discovered the fraud more than six years prior to the filing of the bill

This rule is very clearly stated and positively asserted by Mr Vice Chancellor Wigram, in Blair vs Bromley, 5 Hare 559, 26 Eng Ch 558, in which he says· '' The onus, in the first instance, was upon the Plaintiffs to prove the misrepresentation they alleged to have been made by the him Having proved that in the single case which I have mentioned they have proved enough, until the Defendant shows that the fraud was discovered at a time which bars the right to relief' See 4 Dess R 480 also Danl Ch. P 746, 6 Yerger R 73-4

So in New York it has been held by the Court of Appeals, that the statute of limitations in cases of fraud does not constitute a defence in equity unless it be averred in the answer and also proved that the Plaintiff discovered the facts constituting the fraud beyond the time which bars relief Sears vs. Shafer 2 Selden's R 268, 275

And the same doctrine is clearly recognized by this Court 19 How R 72

This question has also been very learnedly and elaborately considered in South Carolina, and the rule as above laid down fortified and established beyond the possibility of a doubt, by an irresistible train of reason and authority

In the case of Thrower vs. Cureton, 4 Strobart's Eq R 158–9 Chancellor Johnston in a most learned and unanswerable opinion, says   The bill avers that the facts constituting the alleged fraud came to the Plaintiff's knowledge within four years before the filing of the bill   Such an allegation is substantially an averment that the Plaintiff was ignorant of them until that time and I am of opinion that such an averment throws the burden upon the Defendant of proving that the Plaintiff was acquainted with the facts for four years or upwards before the bill was filed otherwise he is not entitled to the benefit of his plea of the statute

The general doctrine is that the statute will not be applied in equity, as a bar to relief against fraud until the facts constituting the fraud are discovered   Cases on this subject present the question whether the Plaintiff, in averring his ignorance of the fraud of which he complains, is to be regarded as offering a reason why the statute should not run against him, or whether his negative averment is not rather to be regarded as the statement of a case which is *prima facie* true. and thereby furnishing the Defendant a fair opportunity to deny the fact, and entitle him to the benefit of the statute, by proving notice or knowledge on the part of the Plaintiff

' If the Plaintiff is obliged to prove his ignorance prior to the time when he admits in his bill that he received information, this is a negative which, in its nature, does not admit of proof, and it follows, that the bar of the statute must be applied by this Court from the date of the fraudulent transaction—contrary to its own maxim, that the statute, in cases of fraud, runs only from the discovery

" 'Ignorance,' says Johnson, J., in the case of Hopkins vs Mazyck, 1 Hill Ch. 251, 'cannot be proved Who can enter into the heart of man and ascertain what knowledge dwells there?' '

" It comes to this, then that if the burden of proof lies on the Plaintiff—if he can relieve himself from the currency of the statute only by proving his ignorance, the protection afforded him by the maxim of this Court, is a mockery; and the Court might as well permit the statute to run from the perpetration of the fraud

" It is a general rule that negatives need not be proved, and the cases in which exceptions are allowed, will be found to be cases in which the nature of the matters involved admits the possibility of proof But ignorance, in its very nature admits of no evidence Vide Gresley's Eq Ev 288–9

" The analogy is strictly to cases where a party pleads or avers a want of notice, of which Eyre vs Dolphin, 2 B. & B 303 cited Gresley's Eq Ev 289, may serve as an example The answer stated that he was a purchaser for valuable consideration, without notice, and, upon going into evidence, the Plaintiff had to prove the notice

" Undoubtedly it is the English practice, that if Plaintiff

charges fraud, and that it was not discovered till within the statutory period, the statute is not a good plea unless the Defendant denies the fraud, or avers that the fraud, if any, was discovered beyond the time limited by the statute. Now if the Defendant contents himself with denying the fraud, and it is found against him, the Plaintiff must be relieved   If, however, the Defendant would avail himself of the statute, he must aver that the fraud was discovered more than six years (with us four years) before bill filed

1   He must swear to the discovery

2   As he avers an affirmative proposition, I think he must prove it

The English practice requires him to plead it, averring the discovery in the plea, and supporting the plea by answer   See Beam's Pleas in Eq 29, 168, 209, and Willis Pleadings, 248, note, Law Lib vol 35.   The averment must be made and proved in order to bring Defendant's case within the statute.—So I infer

"It is true that in *Booth* vs *Warrington*, 1 Br. P. C 455, and in *Wambursee* vs *Kennedy*, 4 Dess R 479, some proof was attempted of the time of discovery, but as might be expected, it amounted to nothing, as such proof always will, and in the latter case, the Chancellor says, ' they state in the bill, that they were not informed until within one year of filing their bill, and there is no proof, on the other side, to induce a belief that they had any earlier knowledge   Says Chancellor Harper in White vs Paussin, Bail Eq 459, 'The rule is notorious that time will not run to protect a fraud until the fraud has been discovered :' (which, by the way, is very much the way in which the doctrine is laid down in So. Sea Co. vs Wymondel, 3 P Wms 144) 'It is true,' continued Chancellor Harper, that the party seeking relief in such a case, must allege that the fraud was discovered within the statutory period before filing the bill The allegation is not strictly susceptible of proof, but it is material to put the Defendant upon proof of discovery ' To the same effect see his observations in Thayer vs Davidson, Bil Eq 420."

And in the case of Shannon vs. White, 6 Rich'd Eq R 100-1, Chancellor Dargan in delivering the unanimous and well considered opinion of the Court of Appeals of South Carolina, in equity causes, says " When the Plaintiff, with the view of evading the bar of the statute of limitations, alleges that the fraud was discovered within four years, (or within a period in which the statute will be no bar,) upon which party does the *onus probandi* lie, of showing the want of notice ? Does it lie with the Plaintiff who alleges the want of notice or with the Defendant who interposes the bar of the statute ? Whether the *onus* lies with the Plaintiff or the Defendant, will in most of cases, seriously affect the result of the issue as to the applicability of the statute

' In the prosecution of this inquiry, and the solution of the question, it will not be improper to resort to the philosophy of evidence

' From the nature of man, and from the circumstances by which he is surrounded, it is rarely possible to establish the negative of any proposition involving an issue of fact in common transactions of life Whether the Plaintiff has had a knowledge of the fraud for more than four years before the filing of his bill, though *he* asserts it, is a negative proposition   And while man has the power of veiling his thoughts, it would be difficult in many, and impossible in most cases, to prove it by evidence   For though it might be shown that he did not have the information from this source or from that—from one or from many individuals, *non constat* that he did not have it from other sources or from other persons   It is a rule in pleading, of almost universal application, that the *onus* is with the party who is interested in establishing the affirmative. And until the affirmative is proved, or *prima facie* proved, it is not necessary for the adverse party to offer any evidence

"The ground upon which the Court of Equity applies the statute of limitations is the *laches* of the plaintiff. He is required to prosecute his claim with a reasonable diligence   But how can *laches* be imparted to him who is ignorant of the fraud? When the Defendant pleads the statute of limitations, the Plaintiff, in an artistic system of pleading might reply, that the statute does not apply, because he had notice only within the statutory period But as we have no replications in this Court, the Plaintiff may allege the want of notice in his bill, in anticipation of the plea.   This must arrest the operation of the statute until the Defendant, who is in the affirmative of the question, by proof, brings his case within its provisions.

"I will conclude what I have to say upon this branch of the subject, by referring to the separate opinion of Chancellor Johnston, in Thrower vs Cureton, 4 Strob. Eq 155, where the authorities are collated

"On the trial then, of this question of notice, it was

incumbent upon the Defendants to prove that the Plaintiffs had notice of the fraud more than four years prior to the filing of the bill "And here it is to be remarked, that it would not be sufficient to prove that the Plaintiff had a suspicion of the fraud. But it is necessary to bring home to the Plaintiff a knowledge of the facts constituting the fraud. Suppose some one were to tell him that a fraud had been committed, it would not be sufficient, unless he were informed of the facts constituting the fraud, or put in the possession of a clew, by which, with a proper diligence he might come to a knowledge of the facts He would not be required to enter into a costly contest, which would end in disappointment and defeat, or to encounter a shadowy and intangible phantom, which was sure to elude his attack " See also 12 Penn St R 49, 53-4

This difference, then, between the rule in equity and the rule at law in Louisiana, as to the burthen of proof in relation to the discovery of the fraud, would be a sufficient ground of itself to sustain the jurisdiction, as the remedy in equity is more complete and less difficult than at law.

For if the party be compelled to resort to the law side of the Court, he must fail in his case, however clearly he may prove the fraud, unless he also proves, in the first instance, and without the Defendant offering any proof whatever, that he discovered the fraud within the time alleged. This, therefore, imposes a double burden on the Plaintiff, and compels him to prove a *negative*, which in any case is extremely difficult and almost impossible For though he prove by a hundred witnesses that they, at such a time, informed him of the acts of fraud, still that would not prove that he did not know it before. The remedy in equity, therefore, in cases of fraud is less difficult and more complete than at law, and this is a sufficient reason for equity assuming a jurisdiction in any case

From this review of the law and the authorities, it is more than apparent that equity has jurisdiction, as the charges made by the bill, and admitted by the naked demurrer, to be true presents a case of fraud of the deepest dye, without one solitary palliating circumstance offered as an excuse to shield or relieve   In such a case we may well say, as was admirably said by this Court in Boyce's Ex's. v Grundy 3, Pet 220. in answer to the objection that the Plaintiff had a remedy at law for the fraud, that, "On this there may be made several remarks , and first that if the facts made out such a case, yet the law, which abhors fraud, does not incline to permit it to purchase indulgence, dispensation or absolution '

III   The statute of limitations as well as lapse of time is not a bar, as the statute, in equity in cases of fraud, only begins to run from discovery

The bill charges and the naked demurrer admits that the Defendant not only perpetrated *all* the various and numerous frauds charged upon the bankrupt law, and the just rights of his creditors, but that he carefully and fraudulently concealed the same from the Plaintiff until within the two years preceding the filing of the bill, and that the Plaintiff, moreover had no knowledge or information whatever calculated to put him on inquiry, and that he was entirely ignorant of the perpetration of any fraud on the part of the bankrupt, until within the two years last past. Upon such a state of facts charged in the bill, and unqualifiedly and unconditionally admitted by the demurrer, without any answer, whatever denying the frauds it seems to us impossible, that a Court of Equity can, for a moment, entertain such a defense as the statute of limitations

The object and spirit of the statute of limitations was the prevention of the perpetration of fraud, and was never designed as a premium and protection to the successful commission and concealment of the same.

And it is for this reason that a Court of Equity will never allow a party who has committed a fraud to avail himself of the statute, but from the time that the party defrauded becomes aware of his rights For until he is made fully aware of the fraud and his rights consequent thereon, he cannot be said to have a cause of action Time, therefore, in equity, in cases of fraud will only begin to run from the discovery of the fraud

This rule was long since established, and has been so repeatedly recognized and enforced, as to be, no longer an open question

It is true, that notwithstanding the statute is not absolutely binding on Courts of Equity, (10 Wheat. 168 per Marshall Ch J Brookshank vs Smith 2 Younge and Coll. Ex Eq. R. 58, Per Alderson, Baron, 1 B Mon R 308 Phalen vs Clark, 19 Conn R. 434; 20 J. R. 47, ib. 583,) yet they adopt it as a reasonable rule to assist their discretion, (not an arbitrary discretion, but a discretion as it is guided by what has been the practice of Courts of Equity, Patterson vs. Gaines et ux. 6 How 584.) and as a general rule apply it to equitable remedies, where the remedy at law in similar cases would be barred   Angell on Lim chap 3, sect 1, p 24, 2d ed

But to this general rule there are well recognized and clearly defined exceptions

I The rule is not applicable to cases of direct *trust* except from the time that full knowledge of the renunciation of the trust is brought home to the *cestui que trust*

II In cases of fraud the statute, in equity, will not begin to run but from the discovery of the same   As Courts of Equity are not embraced by the statute and only apply it in analogy to the remedy at law they never permit it to be applied, when to do so, would be inconsistent with the fixed and uniform principle, upon which the foundations of equity jurisprudence are based, to wit that a party shall never avail himself of any advantage acquired by his own fraud, and which it would therefore be *against conscience* that he should insist upon   Angell on Lim chap 3, sec. 6, p 28, 2d ed., Murray vs Coster, 20 J. R. 583

This was long since the established doctrine in England, which has ever since been uniformly and steadily affirmed, not only in the English Chancery and House of Lords, but in this as well as most of the other Courts of the Union

In the case of Booth vs. Lord Warrington, 4 Bro. Parl. Ca., 163, Tom ed , same case, 1 Bro. P. C 445, where a party had obtained a large sum of money by falsely representing that he had paid or was bound to pay the same for having procured the Plaintiff's marriage with a lady of fortune and the fraud was not discovered until nine years after, when the Plaintiff exhibited his bill to recover the money thus fraudulently obtained, the House of Lords unanimously resolved that the statute of limitations was not a bar, and this ruling has ever since been maintained in England.

In Hoveden vs Lord Annesly, 2 Sch. & Lef 634, Lord Redesdale says· "Fraud is a secret thing and may remain undiscovered   During such time the statute of limitations should not operate, because, until discovery the title to avoid it does not completely arise   A Court of Equity is well warranted in avoiding the transaction, notwithstanding the statute of limitations, for *pending the concealment of the fraud, the statute of limitations ought not in conscience to run, the conscience of the party being so effected that he ought not to be allowed to avail himself of the length of time,* but after the discovery of the fact imputed as fraud the party has a right to avail himself of the statute "

Mr Lewin, in his treatise on Trust and Trustees, 616, has collected many of the earlier English cases, and states the rule as follows ' But no time will cover a fraud *so long as it remains concealed,* for, until discovery, the title to avoid the transaction does not properly arise "

And Alderson, Baron, in the case of Brookshank vs Smith, 2 Younge & Coll Ex. Eq 58, holds this clear and emphatic language " Then, is the statute of limitation a bar to the remedy sought by this bill ? It seems to me that it is not so   The statute does not absolutely bind Courts of Equity ; but they adopt it as a rule to assist their discretion. In cases of fraud, however, they hold that the statute runs from the discovery. because the laches of the Plaintiff commences from that date, on his acquaintance with all the circumstances   In this, Courts of Equity differ from Courts of Law. which are absolutely bound by the words of the statute " Cited in note 3 to 2 St. Eq sec 1521, a 5th ed

In Blair vs Bromley, 5 Hare 542, 26 Eng Ch R. 541, where one of two partners committed a fraud (of which his co-partner was entirely innocent) but which was not discovered until nine years thereafter, and more than six years after the dissolution of the partnership it was held by Mr Vice Chancellor Wigram, that the co-partner was liable for the constructive fraud and that the statute of limitations would only run from the discovery of the fraud And this ruling of the distinguished Vice Chancellor was affirmed on appeal in 1847, in the High Court of Chancery in Blair vs Bromley, 2 Phil. 354. 22 Eng Ch R. 353

In this case Lord Chancellor Cottenham says ' In the present case, the misrepresentation continued until the fraud was discovered the case therefore, according to Sir William Grant. is the same as if on that day, the fund having been previously invested had been called in and received by the Messrs Bromley in which case, there could not have been any question as to the statute of limitations.'

' I am, therefore of opinion that William Bromley's partner though he had no knowledge, or means of knowledge of his misrepresentation, would have been affected by this equity arising from it and that time did not begin to run against the Plaintiff's right until the discovery of the fraud 22 Eng Ch 359, 360

And in the case of Bowen vs Evans, 2 House of Lords Cases, (by Clarke & Finnelly) 257, the House of Lords held, that if a fraud is proved, *no lapse of time* will protect the parties to it, or those claiming through them, against the jurisdiction of a Court of Equity, and in that case it is immaterial by what machinery or contrivance the fraudulent transactions may have been effected; whether by a decree in equity or judgment at law, or otherwise.

From this review of the English cases it seems that the rule that the statute, in cases of fraud, will only commence to run from discovery, has been uniformly asserted and maintained from an early period down to the present time.

In this country, too, the same doctrine has been repeatedly recognized and enforced by the most learned of Courts as well as by the most illustrious and distinguished jurist of this or any other land

In Shannon vs. White, 6 Rich'd Eq. R 101, the Court of Appeals of South Carolina in Equity causes, well says· "The ground upon which the Court of Equity applies the statute of limitations is the *laches* of the Plaintiff. He is required to prosecute his claim with a reasonable diligence   But how can *laches* be imputed to him who is ignorant of the fraud?"

Judge Story states the rule as follows: "Courts of Equity not only act in obedience and analogy to the statute of limitations in proper cases, but they also interpose in many cases to prevent the bar of the statutes, where it would be inequitable and unjust   Thus, for example, if a party has perpetrated a fraud which has not been discovered until the statutable bar may apply to it, at law, Courts of Equity will interpose and remove the bar out of the way of the injured party   *A fortiori they will not allow such a bar to prevail by mere analogy,* to suits in equity, where it would be in furtherance of a manifest injustice." 2 St Eq., sec. 1521 A like rule is laid down in Angell on Limitations, chap. 3, sec 6, p. 28 See also on the distinction between the rule in Courts of Law and Equity on this subject Angell on Lim. p 188, chap. 18, sec. 1, 2d ed.

In New York this question has been carefully examined in the case of Troup vs Smith, 20 J R 45, top page In the opinion of the Court, delivered by Chief Justice Spencer, it is said : "There is a marked and manifest distinction between a plea of the statute of limitations in a Court of Law and a Court of Equity " And after quoting with approbation the language of Lord Redesdale, in 2 Sch. & Lef. 634, Chief Justice Spencer says· "Courts of Equity not being bound by the statute any further than they have seen fit to adopt its provisions as a reasonable rule, and then only in analogy to the general doctrines of that Court, are perfectly right in saying, that a party cannot in good conscience avail himself of the statute, when by his own fraud he has prevented the other party from coming to a knowledge of his rights, until within six years prior to the commencement of the suit "

And in Murray vs Coster, 20 J R 576, 582, Chief Justice Spencer again says· "It is to be observed that, strictly speaking, the statute of limitations does not apply to a Court of Equity That Court has adopted it as a fit and convenient rule, but with its own restrictions which are, that in cases of fraud and trust, it shall not apply." And at page 585 he holds this positive language "In cases of trusts, and fraud, peculiarly, appropriately, and exclusively the objects of equity jurisdiction, according to the established doctrine, the statute cannot be pleaded "

So Judge Story in sec. 1521, a. 2 St Eq. has laid down the rule as follows "The question often arises in cases of fraud and mistake, and acknowledgements of debts, and of trust and charges on lands for payment of debts, under what circumstances and at what time, the bar of the statute of limitations begins to run In general it may be said, that the rule of Courts of Equity is, that the cause of action or suit, arises, when and as soon, as the party has a right to apply to a Court of Equity for relief In cases of *fraud*, or *mistake*, it *will begin to run from the time of the discovery*, of *such fraud*, or mistake, *and not before.*"

In Phalen vs Clark, 19 Conn R 421, the Supreme Court of Errors of Connecticut, after a thorough discussion, and on the most mature deliberation, where the Defendant, having perpetrated a fraud to the injury of the Plaintiff, which if prosecuted in due season, would have entitled him to relief, carefully and fraudulently concealed from the Plaintiff all knowledge of the truth of the facts in question, for such a period, that the statute would bar a remedy in a Court of Law, held that the Plaintiff, under the circumstances, was entitled to relief in equity, and that the statute of limitations would only commence to run from the discovery of the fraud.

At page 435 of this authority, Chief Justice Church, after reviewing the authorities and recognizing the rule that equity recognizes and enforces the statute in many cases of both legal and equitable remedies, said· "While we concede the full effect of the foregoing principles, we deny their application, by Courts of Equity, to cases of fraud like the present—cases where a Defendant,

by his own fraudulent acts and representations, has allay-
ed all reasonable suspicion of his original fraud, and thus
attempted to obtain an unconscientious advantage, by
lapse of time. To yield such advantage to a Defendant,
would be to disregard the most prominent ground of
equitable jurisdiction, and to permit the hands of that
Court to become bound, by the very frauds against which
it ought to afford relief."

And the same rule will be found to be fully and unqualifiedly recognized in the following authorities. 1
Curtis C C R 230; 6 Richd Eq R 100-1, 4 Strob, Eq.
R. 155, Bail Eq 459, 4 Dess 479-80, 1 Mc Ch R 314,
3 Dess. 223, 12 Geo. R 371, 375-8; 8 Geo. R. 511, ib. 1;
4 Kelly R 308, 12 Penn. R. 49, 53-4, 8 Watts 12, 1
Watts 401, 1 Blackf R 77; 2 Sum R 491, 551. 563
1Wood & Min R 111–12, 3 3 Leigh's R 732, 735,
738, 3 Murphy 593; 6 Yerger 69, 3 J. J. Mar. 15; 1 J J
Mar 40-1, 3 Mon 40, 4 J J Mar. 77, 1 B Mon. 308-9.
4 Dan. 226

In Sherwood vs Sutton, 5 Mason, 143, Mr Justice
Story reviews the decisions at length, and held that fraud
would avoid the statute both at law and in equity At
page 154 of the above authority, he says : "The statute
of limitations was mainly intended to suppress fraud, by
preventing fraudulent and unjust claims from starting up
at great distances of time, when the evidence might no
longer be within the reach of the other party, by which they
could be repelled It ought not, then, to be so construed
as an instrument to encourage fraud, if it admits of any
other reasonable interpretation, and cases of fraud, therefore, form an implied exception, to be acted upon by

Courts of Law and Equity, according to the nature of their respective jurisdictions "

In Breckenridge vs Churchill, 3 J. J Mar 15, the Court said "Where chancery and common law courts have concurrent jurisdiction, time is, generally, as inexorable a bar in chancery as at law Fraud is an exception; for, limitation to a bill for fraud will not commence till the discovery of the fraud."

And in Gates and wife vs Jacob et al, 1 B Mon R 308-9, Chief Justice Robertson well says: "It is historically as well as intrinsically evident that, long after the enactment of the statute of limitation of *James in England*, Courts of Equity began, voluntarily to adopt the statute by *analogy*, but with such equitable qualifications as to effectuate its spirit and policy, and prevent the pervertion of its letter, and consequently, the following rules have been established in equity, by long practice and repeated recognitions : 1st, in cases of concurrent jurisdiction, as it would be unreasonable to allow the remedy in equity after that at law, upon the same right, had been barred by the statute, the limitation will be inflexibly applied in a Court of Equity, precisely as it operates at law, with the *exception* of cases of fraud, and probably mistake, in which the reason of the statute, contrary in this respect to its letter, *dates the bar from the discovery before which there could have been no suit.*"

So in 10 Wheat. 174, Chief Justice Marshall *held* that the statute of limitations and lapse of time was not a bar in cases of fraud or disabilities.

And in Miched et al vs Girod et al, 4 How. (S C.) 561, this Court says: "There is no rule in equity which excludes the consideration of circumstances, and in a case of actual fraud, we believe no case can be found in which a Court of Equity has refused to give relief within the lifetime of either of the parties upon whom the fraud is proved, or within thirty years after it has been discovered, or become known to the party whose rights are affected by it "

So in Hallet et al vs Collins, 10 How. R. 174, 187, where the party had complicated and covered up the title, so that the parties would not have known their rights if the facts had been laid before them. although there had been great delay in bringing the suit, yet the Court said " The absence of the complainant from the State, and the late *discovery of the fraud,* fully account for the delay and apparent laches in prosecuting his claim "

Again, in the late case of Moore vs Green et al , 19 How R. 69, 72 Mr. Justice McLean in delivering the unanimous opinion of the Court, uses this decisive and conclusive language " Where fraud is alleged as a ground to set aside a title, the statute does not begin to run until the fraud is discovered "

And in Louisiana, the law is well settled, that although right of action may accrue or exist at a certain period, yet prescription does *not* begin to run until that right can be exercised, because no delay can be imputed to one before that time, and hence the maxim in the jurisprudence of that State, "*contra non valentem agere, non currit præscriptio.*' 2 N. S 432-3; 7 N S 481; 12 Mart 76-7, 3 L R 219. 221, 4 Ann 170-1

"All acts of hindrance—*voies de fait et impechemens,* (says the Court in 4 Ann. R. 170,) coming from the debtor, which deprive the creditor of the remedy and forum contemplated at the time of the contract suspend prescription." 2 Troplong, Prescription 725

We may well say then with Judge Porter in 3 La R. 221, that this Defendant "certainly opposes with a bad grace, prescription to a demand, which through his own fault the creditor was prevented from enforcing earlier by suit"

With such an overwhelming weight of the highest authority in support of the position that in cases of fraud the statute will only begin to run from the discovery of the same, we are more than confident that we might here safely rest this branch of the case

But as the case of Buckner and Stanton, applts vs Calcote, 28 Miss. R. 432, will no doubt be pressed on the Court as holding a different doctrine, and as being directly applicable to the case before the Court, we would respectfully say that it will require but a brief notice (if in fact any is necessary) to show that it is not only at variance with former rulings of the same Court, but above all that it is wholly unsupported by any authority whatever.

Now it is true the high Court of Mississippi, on a bill specifically charging fraud and all of which charges were admitted by the demurrer without any answer whatever, denying the fraud or the discovery of the same within eighteen months, as charged, did decide that the statute was a bar

But with due consideration we must be permitted to say, that this decision, of that Court, is *sui generis*, and that there is no authority throughout the civilized world that supports such a doctrine

It is wholly at war with every equitable principle, and is more remote from the orbit in which a Court of Equity has hitherto moved, than the orb of Jupiter from that of our earth

How a Court professing to sit as a Court of Equity, could thus fly off at a tangent from every equitable rule and principle, we have ever been at a loss to comprehend, unless we assume (as was no doubt the case) that it was a foregone conclusion, without consideration or research.

For even had the Court been guided by the light of its own former experience, it must have seen the departure it was about to make, and the chaos and confusion into which it was rushing

And that this criticism may not seem unjust, we desire specially to call the attention of this Court to the case of Livermore, vs Johnson, 27 Missp. R 284, to show in the *first place*, that in cases of fraud the statute in equity will only begin to run from the discovery of the fraud, and in the *second place*, to show that where a bill charging fraud contains an allegation that the fraud was only discovered within such time as would exclude the bar of the statute, a demurrer to the bill *cannot* be sustained

At page 289 of this last authority, Chief Justice Smith, in speaking on the first point says · " It has long been the settled rule in England that when a party has been kept in ignorance of his rights by the fraud of the person sought to be charged, the statute shall not begin to run until after the fraud has been discovered The reason assigned why the statute bar will not be applied in a Court of Equity in a case of that character is, that it would be a violation of the principles of natural justice to permit a party to avail himself of lapse of time as a bar to the suit who has by fraud kept concealed the rights of the complainant and has thereby delayed him in the assertion of those rights. Hoveden vs Lord Annesly 2 Sch & Lef. R 634 Such is without doubt the doctrine of Courts of Equity in this country, Story's Equity 738 Lewin on Trustees 617 Carter vs Murry, 5 J Ch R 522 And such unquestionably is the law in this country, Angell on Lim (and the cases cited,) p 188 In Hoveden vs Lord Annesly 2 Sch & Lef 634 Lord Redesdale in his very able and elaborate judgment says Fraud is a secret thing and may remain undiscovered During such time the statute of limitations should not operate, because until discovery the title to avoid it does not completely arise Again in the same case page 634 a Court of Equity is well warranted in avoiding the transaction, notwithstanding the statute of limitations for *pending the concealment of the fraud, the statute of limitations ought not in conscience to run, the conscience of the party being so **affected** that he ought not to be allowed to avail himself of the length of time* but after the discovery of the fact imputed as fraud the party has a right to avail himself of the statute

With such a clear recognition as this in favor of the doctrine that the statute in case of fraud will only run from discovery is it not surprising that a Court should suddenly fly to the opposite extreme, to shelter and protect admitted fraud, treachery and deceit '

But to proceed In this same case this same Court, at pages 290, 292, on the *second point,* remarks In cases in which a plea of the statute is interposed the rule as laid down by Chancellor Kent in Goodrich vs Pendle-

8

ton, 3 J. Ch R. 385, is, that the equitable circumstances charged in the bill and which will prevent the operation of the statute, must be denied by the answer as well as by the plea; and the answer must be full and clear, and contain a particular denial of the charges or it will not be effective to sustain the plea "

"The rule on this subject is well settled Where the bill charges a fraud, and that the fraud was not discovered till within six years before the filing the bill, the statute is not a good plea, unless the Defendant deny the fraud or aver that the fraud, if any, was discovered six years before filing the bill Mitford, Ch. Plead. 269, Goodrich vs. Pendleton, 3 J. Ch R 385, Lewin on Trustees, 617 It follows, therefore that the plea was bad, and should not have been sustained See also 5 Smedes & Mar 20 5 How. (Miss) R 365, 12 S & Mar, 191, 216, all of which fully recognize the same doctrine, that a naked demurrer to a bill charging fraud cannot be sustained

With such an unqualified recognition of the well established rule in equity, by the Court in Mississippi how was it possible for it to rule the very opposite in the case of Buckner & Stanton vs. Calcote? and we may ask, how is it possible for this or any other Court to regard it as authority? For let it be borne in mind, that the bill in that case expressly and explicitly charged, that all the frauds specified had been discovered within the eighteen months preceding the filing of the bill, and further charged, that neither the complainant nor his assignor had any knowledge or information whatever calculated to put them on inquiry until within the preceding eighteen months Now, according to *every* equitable authority and principle, that was all that was necessary to prevent the bar of the statute on a naked demurrer. Under such circumstances, the Defendants, according to the oft and well established rule, were bound to answer the charges of fraud, and could only interpose the statute as a bar by replying, that the fraud, if any, had been discovered more than six years before the filing of the bill Such being the undoubted law, the Court in Mississippi was wholly unwarranted in sustaining the demurrer and dismissing the bill, and its decision in that case cannot but be regarded as a total overthrow of the most clearly defined and well established rule in equity which is that, where there are equitable circumstances stated in the bill, which are sufficient to take the case out of the statute the Defendant cannot demur or plead the statute without an answer denying the fraud, and averring that the fraud, if any, was discovered beyond a time which bars relief Story's Eq P sects 684, 754, 3 J Ch 384, 7 J Ch 134 Lewin on Trustees 617, 8 Geo. R 108-9, 4 Dess 480, 2 Danl Ch. P 736, 6 Yerg 69, 93-4, Hoveden vs Lord Annesly, 2 Sch & Lef 635, South Sea Company vs. Wymonsell, 3 P Wms 143, Booth vs Lord Warrington, 4 Bro. P C. 163, Tomb ed., 4 W C C 639 3 Mylne & Craig R. 475, 2 Young & Coll Ex Eq R 58; 3 ib 683; Ang Limit Ch 26, sect 12; Welford's Eq P 391, 393.

Not only then is the decision in the case of Buckner & Stanton vs Calcote not warranted from this review of the authorities, but it is wholly unsupported and unsustained by a solitary authority cited in the same And to our mind it is really surprising that any Court could so pervert or misconstrue authorities

In the case of Farnum vs Brooks 9 Pick. R 212, (and which is cited by the Mississippi Court as authority for its opinion) the bill was filed after a lapse of nearly twenty years, by the administrator *de bonis non* to set aside a compromise settlement and receipt in full for $60,000, on the suggestion and charge of misrepresentation and a fraudulent concealment and which settlement was made by the administrators of the intestate shortly after his death by way of a full and final adjustment and settlement of a long and complicated account of co-partnership on the recommendation and advice of an experienced book-keeper whom they themselves employed to examine the books and papers, and the Court held that as there was no foundation for the charges of fraud and misrepresentation and that as "the books themselves together with the papers from which the errors were detected, were within the control of the administrators, and were actually examined as far as they wished, by a person in whom they placed confidence " the statute, under these circumstances, would be a bar to the re-opening of the account but sustained the bill to correct mistakes, as the Defendant in his answer admitted there were some errors

This case then, surely, is no authority for this most extraordinary doctrine of the Mississippi Court, that the statute is a bar to a fraud But on the contrary, it is entirely opposed to such a dangerous and unwarrantable doctrine, and is in strict conformity and harmony with the repeated decisions in Massachusetts on this subject

For Chief Justice Parker in this very case, 9 Pick 244-5 after stating that *trusts* were not within the statute well and admirably says ' The other ground upon which the

statute of limitations is allowed to be avoided is *fraud*,
and we do not discern, upon examination of the authorities cited, any material difference in the principle when
applied in chancery and when at law. The common law
allows fraud, if not discovered until within six years before action brought to be a good answer to the statute
as in Homer vs Fish 1 Pick 435. Courts of Equity do
no more, except that they do not in all cases require a
recent discovery of the fraud to repel the statute. The
general doctrine, however is that the lapse of six years
after the discovery is a bar.

Such is the language of the Court in the case of Farnum
vs Brooks, and yet the Court in Mississppi cites this case
as authority for its opinion that the statute is a bar to a
fraud discovered within six years when it positively and
explicitly discountenances any such doctrine and expressly
holds that the statute in cases of fraud will only run from
discovery.

So the case of Johnson vs Johnson 5 Alab (N S) R
90 is in no respect an authority for the opinion of the
Mississippi Court, but in principle is directly the other
way.

That was a case where the Plaintiff, a distributee, filed
a bill against his father's administrator for an account and
settlement. The defense was that after the complainant
became of full age the Defendant accounted with him and
fully paid him, etc, and that he acquiesced in this settlement for upwards of eleven years until the filing of the
bill, and the Court *held* that, as the trust was destroyed
by the contract of the parties and as the allegation of the
discovery of the fraud (which was that he was not advised

ot the same until long after the settlement,) was too *gene-ral* and *vague* to be the basis of any action in a Court of justice, and moreover as the evidence showed that complainant had the same knowledge of all the facts at the time of the settlement or soon after, that he had at the time of filing of the bill that therefore, the same could not be maintained

Of course then there was no excuse for the delay and consequently no ground for relief This case therefore is no authority for this new doctrine of the Mississippi Court And it is worthy of note and observation that the cases in Massachusetts and Alabama were on bill and answer and not on demurrer and moreover, it is clear that they both recognize the doctrine that the statute in cases of fraud only runs from the time the party either discovers the fraud or has *full* knowledge of the means of ascertaining his rights How then can such authorities be fairly used in support of such a doctrine as that laid down in Buckner and Stanton vs Calcote? But the most striking and palpable perversion and disregard of authority by the Mississippi Court in that opinion is, the case of Kane vs Bloodgood, 7 J Ch 90.

Now that case is directly opposed to the opinion of the High Court of Mississippi and is one of the very best of authorities for the opposite doctrine For in that case (7 J Ch 122-3.) Chancellor Kent says It is equally said that fraud, as well as trust is not within the statute, and it is well settled that the statute does not run until the discovery of the fraud; for the title, to avoid it does not arise until then and pending the concealment of it, the statute ought not in conscience to run ; but after the discovery of the fact imputed as fraud, the statute runs as in other cases 'This was the true ground of the case of Booth vs. Lord Warrington 1 Bro P. C 455 and this was the rule declared in the case of the South Sea Company vs Wymondsell, 3 P W. 143, and Lord Redesdale in the case in which I have so long dwelt approves of the rule "

From this extract it is seen that the Court in Mississippi is not only wholly unsupported by Chancellor Kent but that he holds a directly opposite doctrine and such as is consistent with adjudged cases It is therefore strange that the distinguished Chancellor's opinion should have been so misapplied. But it is said that Homer sometimes nodded, and it is but charitable to suppose that the Court in Mississippi, when it pronounced that most extraordinary opinion and so misapplied Chancellor Kent, must have been under the influence of some strange hallucination

But again. if we notice the Mississippi case a little farther its departure from well recognized principles will if possible, be rendered more apparent In that case it was said that it was not charged that the bankrupts, after obtaining their discharges, had used any positive acts of fraud towards the complainant, and that, ' for aught that appears in the bill, the frauds might have been as well discovered by the exercise of due diligence within eighteen months after their commission, as within eighteen months before the filing of the bill. From their nature, as charged, they were open, and entirely capable at all times of being detected. The proceedings in bankruptcy were open to examination, and all parties inter-

ested were notified to contest them, if they thought fit to
do so. Thus all parties were placed at arms length, and
each upon his own rights with nothing of confidence or
trust existing between them '

Such is the unparalleled language and sentiment of the
Mississippi Court ' It says for aught that appeared, the
frauds might have been discovered within eighteen months
after the bankrupts obtained their discharge

Now the bill in that case positively charged that the
frauds which consisted of payments, preferences etc , in
contemplation of bankruptcy were wholly unknown to
the complainant and that he had no knowledge or information of any fact or facts calculated to put him on inquiry until within eighteen months of the filing of the
bill This is all that was necessary to prevent the bar of
the statute For it is a well known rule of pleading, that
a naked demurrer admits not only the truth of all the
facts charged in the bill, but also all that can be legitimately deduced and inferred from the facts so charged
and admitted

It was therefore disingenuous for the Court to say '' for
aught that appears the fraud might have been discovered
before '

The case was not before the Court in that aspect nor
could the Court legitimately make such a deduction, when
the party by demurring had admitted the contrary, as
charged in the bill   6 How R 118, 3 McLean 243, 421

Nor was the Court justified in saying, that the matters
of fraud might have been investigated in bankruptcy How
could payments, preferences, etc , be a matter of redress
or litigation in bankruptcy, when the parties, (as was al-

leged and admitted by the demurrer) had no knowledge
or information in relation to the same which was even
calculated to put them on inquiry ' The very statement
of the case refutes the position assumed And the statement that the parties stood at arms length in bankruptcy,
and that there was no relation of trust or confidence between them is as dangerous as it is unsound, both in
morals and in law Neither the letter, spirit, or policy of
the bankrupt or any other law give countenance or support to this most startling and extraordinary doctrine

Indeed the authorities are ample to show, that any concealment by which a party obtains an unfair advantage
of another, (although there is no relation of confidence or
trust between them) will deprive such party of all the ad-
vantages thus obtained Martin vs Morgan, 1 Brod &
Bing R 289 Pidcock vs Bishop, 3 B & Cres 605

And besides, when a bankrupt goes voluntarily into
Court, and compels his creditors to come into bankruptcy
he does not, in the eye of the law, stand in hostile array
to the rights and interest of his creditors He stands
there as the agent of all in making as the *law exacts* of
him, an honest and fair surrender *under oath*, of all of
his property for the common benefit of his creditors, and
if he fails to disclose the truth his discharge will be held
invalid 1 St Eq § 217

The Court and the creditors therefore, have a right to
presume he has acted honestly and fairly towards both
the creditors and the law And if he acts fraudulently
in not making a fair surrender it does not lie in his
mouth (much less a Court of Equity for him, to say

9

you should not have trusted in my *sworn* representations that I had made an honest and fair surrender

For the rule of law is clear, that where a party makes a false and fraudulent representation in a matter of interest to another, he shall not be permitted afterwards to say, in order to escape liability, that you ought not to have relied on my statements and representations, but should have inquired for yourself, as you had information to put you on inquiry

To such a one, too, we might well reply in the language of this Court, in Boyce Ex's vs Grundy, 3 Pet 218 which is as follows "It is said that it ought to have put him on inquiry, but he was in possession of Mr Boyce's positive assurance to the contrary, and had a right to rely on that assurance without inquiry'

So the creditors in bankruptcy, being in possession of the bankrupt's sworn and positive statement that he had made an honest and fair surrender, had a right to rely on the same, and were under no obligation to go seeking after supposed or perhaps imaginary frauds

For, as is well said by the Supreme Court in Illinois 'If the complainant was too confiding, it is not for the party who has betrayed that confidence to reproach him with, or take advantage of it' 2 Gillman (Ill) R 388

In Reynell vs Sprye, Sprye vs Reynell, on a rehearing before the Lords Justices, Lord Cranworth, L J, after adverting to the fact that the Defendant not only left the complainant at perfect liberty to consult his friends and professional advisers, but even on several occasions recommended him to do so, and proceeding to state that if the relief sought rested on mere mistake instead of *misi epresentations of fact*, that the party might perhaps be excused, said "But no such question can arise in a case like the present, where one contracting party has intentionally misled the other by describing his rights as being different from what he knew them really to be In such a case it is no answer to the charge of imputed fraud to say, that the party alleged to be guilty of it recommended the other to take advice, or even put into his hands the means of discovering the truth. However negligent the party may have been to whom the incorrect statement has been made, yet that is a matter affording no ground of defense to the other For no man can complain that another has too implicitly relied on the truth of what he has himself stated This principle was fully recognized in the case of Dobell vs Stevens, 3 B. & C 625, referred to by my learned brother in in the course of the argument" 8 Hare, 268, 32 Eng Ch R. 267 *in note*

So Sir James Wigram, Vice Chancellor, also, in the above case, where the party had made certain statements and failed to correct them, on discovering his error, said "In such case, it is not enough for Sprye to say, that the Plaintiff had the means of knowing the truth; he is bound to show that his attention was actually called to it." 8 Hare 258, 32 Eng. Ch 257 See also 11 Mess. & Well R 116, Smith's Mer L. 461

And in Ranger vs. The Great Western Railway Co, 27 Eng. L. & Eq. R. 44, in the House of Lords, we find this strong and forcible language " In these circumstances, I think it is impossible to believe that there was anything like contrivance to mislead the appellant or any other contractor ; and it is clear that the appellant, if there was no fraud, was bound to satisfy himself on the subject , for the specifications of the proposed works, submitted to him before the tender was made, expressly stipulates that the contractor must satisfy himself of the nature of the soil and of all matters which can in any way influence his contract. This, though of course it would not absolve the Company from the consequences of any fraudulent contrivances to mislead, yet certainly. in the absence of fraud threw on the appellant the obligation of judging for himself."

If, therefore, the Company under such stipulations in the above case could not and would not have been excused, had there been any fraud, how is it possible for a Court of Equity to make such an excuse as is made by the Court in Mississippi for interposing the statute as a bar to protect a fraudulent bankrupt ?

Such then being the law as laid down both by this Court and the Lords Justices and House of Lords, in England, in regard to the force and effect of representations made by a party, it is very clear, that a bankrupt, when he returns his schedules and inventories under oath, cannot be viewed as standing at arms-length with his creditors, nor can it be said, in order to shield and protect him by the statute of limitations, in his fraud, that his creditors had no right to rely on his sworn representations to the Court as well as to themselves. His sworn representations to the Court and his creditors make it unnecessary for them to inquire after fraud, and they may rely on his having sworn the truth without any fear or danger of being barred by the

[To be inserted after line 2, page 69]

For not only has it been admirably said by Chief Justice Williams, 2 Green's (Iowa) R 75, that he had not been able to find any authority requiring a party to be vigilant and cautious in guarding against fraud, and that on his failure so to do he would be considered as in default, and bound by his neglect and acquiescence, but it has also been well and expressly held by Mr. Justice Dewey, in 13 Met 63-4, that a creditor of a bankrupt may not only prove his claim and take a dividend in bankruptcy on the assumption that the bankrupt has made an honest and fair surrender, and that if fraud should afterwards appear, that he would be entitled to relief, but that he has, moreover, no right to suspect fraud on the part of the bankrupt, and to govern his conduct accordingly, because no one has a right to presume that another has violated the law The Mississippi case, then, is clearly not law   And may it please your Honors, we have no doubt but that when this cause shall have been decided, this Mississippi case will fade away and disappear forever, like one of those erratic heavenly orbs which has · flamed in the forehead of the morning sky, sunk away in the distance, and disappeared in a blaze of light far, far off, beyond the pillarless vault of heaven

This is no fancy sketch—no penciling of the imagination For e en had we a poet s pen, and could we pluck all the varied hues from the "Bow of promise and write the law on this subject on the parchment of heaven, we could not read in clearer or more intelligible language than we now behold in the authorities, that the statute in cases of fraud will only run from the discovery of the same statute of limitations of their right to avoid his discharge, if at any time the fraud should afterwards appear

For a party who perpetrates a fraud is held, in Equity to be a trustee for the party defrauded   2 How. S. C. R 649-50, 2 Sch. & Lef. 633   And the rule is, that if a trust be constituted by the fraud of one of the parties, or arises from a decree of a Court of Equity, the possession of the trustee becomes adverse, and the statute will only run from the time the fraud was *discovered*

Chancellor Desaussure in 4 Dess. 479, says   'This transaction then being considered fraudulent and raising a trust, we come to the question whether, in such case the statute of limitations is allowed to operate

'I take the law on that subject to be as follows As a rule, the statute of limitations does not operate in cases of fraud and of trusts but as soon as the fraud is discovered, it commences to run   This doctrine is laid down in the case of Booth vs. Earl of Warrington, decided, in the House of Lords with the assistance of all the judges See ib 480

And in 1 McCords Ch. R 314, it is held that trust and fraud are excepted from the operation of the statute upon purely equitable principles

In Thompson vs. Blair, 3 Murphy (N C) R 393 Chief Justice Taylor says

' If a party is to be construed a trustee by the decree of a Court of Equity, founded in fraud or the like, his possession is adverse and the statute of limitations will run from the time that the circumstances of the fraud were discovered   A fraudulent transaction, from the secrecy with which it is usually conducted, may remain for a long time unknown to the injured party, and it would be unconscientious to allow the Defendant to avail himself of the statute during such a period '

And in Harrison vs Acock et al. 8 Geo. R 68, 70--1, Mr Justice Warner says 'If a party is to be construed a *trustee*, by a decree of a Court of Equity, founded on *fraud*, his possession is *adverse* from the time the circumstances of the fraud were discovered, and the statute of limitations will run from that time ' See also Mr Justice Lumpkin s elaborate and well considered opinion in 12 Geo R 371 in which he concurs with Judge Story's views in Sherwood vs. Sutton, 5 Mason 143 that the statute only runs from the discovery of the fraud, 2 Sch & Lef 633, 2 Dan'l Ch P. 735-6, 20 Mo R 541

The principle upon which this rule is founded is, that the statute runs from every new right of action or suit which accrues to the Plaintiff, and that the discovery of the fraud gives to such Plaintiff a new right 2 Dan'ls Ch P 736-7, 2 Sch. & Lef 630 20 Mo R 541; 3 Murphy's (N C) R 393

And the time within which the statute against a fraud is complete, must be governed by the nature of the claim against which it is set up 6 Richd Eq R 144. 20 Mo R 541; 16 Ark R 144

According to this rule then, the plea of prescription is inapplicable (article 3508 of the Civil Code limits suits on bills and notes to *five years*) as the bill charges, and the demurrer admits that all the frauds were discovered within the two years preceding the filing of the bill The plea of prescription then must be wholly unavailing. Nor can the conclusiveness of this position be avoided by attempting to show that this proceeding is an action of nullity of judgment, and therefore governed by a different period of prescription

For, in the first place, an action of nullity will only lie in the Court which rendered the judgment 1 Hennin's Dig 792 5

And again, it is well settled that where a party has different remedies, in relation to the same matter, one of which is barred and the other is not, he may successfully pursue that which is not barred 20 Mo R 482, 11 Conn R 160, 1 Alab R 744, and authorities cited . 2 Alab 331 2 S & Mar R 687, 5 ib 651; 16 Ark R 145

Even then if the bankrupt act was in force, and the direct action to annul the discharge was barred, still according to the principle of the above authorities. we would have the undoubted right to pursue our remedy to recover our debt, which we have seen is not barred by less than five years

For on no principle whatever can this suit be regarded as an action of nullity

The statements in the bill which anticipate the defense of a discharge, should the same be set up in bar, (as it must be, even if absolutely stated in the bill Mitford's Eq P 241. 5 U S Stat 444) only supplies the place of a special replication at law and has uniformly been so regarded Foley vs. Hill, 3 Mylne & Craig 475 14 Eng Ch 476, 483; Mitford's Eq P 242-3.

If the suit had been on the law side of the Court, and a special replication put in to the plea of the certificate, there surely could not have been any pretense for saying that the suit was an action of nullity or that as a direct action to annul the discharge was barred, that therefore the action for the recovery of the debt must also be regarded as barred. For a party may attack a judgment for fraud when opposed to him, by way of exception, and such proceeding is not an action of nullity. 2 How. R 647, 6 How R 583

And moreover it is expressly held in Louisiana, that though a direct action to annul a judgment obtained by fraud may be prescribed, yet it may be attacked and avoided in a collateral proceeding when opposed to the party by way of exception. 11 La R 521

Judge Bullard, at page 532 of this authority says: 'If the Defendant meant to say that the Plaintiff's direct action to annul the judgment of separation on the ground of fraud and collusion being prescribed, he was also prescribed from offering evidence to impeach it when opposed to him by way of exception. we think the proposition equally untenable.

As the charges of fraud in the bill then are nothing more nor less than a special replication at law to the plea or exception of a discharge, it is very clear that this suit cannot be regarded as an action of nullity, and that consequently even if the direct action to annul the discharge were prescribed still that is no objection to the party pursuing his legal remedy to recover his debt as the above authorities fully show.

The plea of prescription must therefore be overruled.

Having thus shown that the statute of limitations is not a bar, it will not be necessary to say much as to the further objection of lapse of time.

On principle as well as authority it would seem that

lapse of time as such, cannot be pleaded or assigned as a cause of demurrer

In 1 Green's (N J) R 68, this subject was elaborately and well considered, and the Court expressly *held* that lapse of time. *as such* could not be pleaded but only that of which it was the evidence

So in Wisner vs Barnet, 4 W C C R 639, Mr Justice Washington says "Where the Defendant means to rely, not upon the *act of limitations* as a bar, but upon *length of time* upon which to raise a presumption against the Plaintiff, he undoubtedly cannot do so by demurrer Belorame vs Brown 3 Brown's C C 646 Edsell vs Buchanan, 2 Ves Jun 83. 4 Browns C. C 254

And the reason of this rule (which is that as lapse of time only operates by way of presumptive evidence, it would, on demurrer, present an inference of fact instead of an inference of law, which is not allowable) is very clearly and forcibly stated and fully recognized in Mitford's Eq P 212, 213

But even were the rule otherwise lapse of time cannot be relied on in this case as the party has set up the statute of limitations as a bar

Lapse of time in equity only applies where there is no statute applicable to the case and none is relied on by the Defendant

But when there is a statute which applies, lapse of time will not be a bar *in a less period* than that of the statute

Mr Lewin, in his Treatise on Trustees, 618, says "As a general rule, the Court presumes, after a lapse of twenty years, but when there is a statuable bar at law and of a different period, the Courts will not entertain a pre-

10

sumption within a less time than the period fixed by the statute ' And the same rule is held in the following authorities. 9 Geo R 243. 3 P Wm 283, 20 Mo R 155, 10 Ohio R 498; 2 Jac & W 141

If, then we have shown (as we are confident we have,) that the statute is not a bar, lapse of time cannot be a bar

And, moreover, where there are circumstances (as the late discovery of the fraud) stated in the bill, which explain and account for the delay a party most clearly cannot rely on lapse of time on demurrer

For lapse of time when there are circumstances *explaining the delay, is no bar to relief in equity*, though there may have been great delay in bringing the suit 1 B Mon 309, 4 Munf R 332, 342-3. 4 Hawk's Law and Eq. R 412, 419, 5 Wend 296, 10 J R 417. Toplis vs Baker 2 Cox's Cases 119, 123, 13 Pick 400, 12 J R 254, 2 Met 28, 1 Story's R 109 118 2 Ball & B 433. 2 St Eq p 1023 in n 7th ed , 28 Eng Ch 24

As the delay in bringing forward the bill, then, is fully accounted for namely, the late discovery of the fraud, lapse of time is no objection

For, as is well said by Mr Lewin on Trustees, 619 " The Court cannot *presume* a person to have abandoned his right so long as he remains in *ignorance* of it or labors under a *mistake* "

And indeed it has been expressly ruled by this Court as well as others, that a demurrer to a bill charging fraud with circumstances explaining the delay, cannot be sustained, there must be an answer denying the fraud 6 How S. C R 114, ib. 163, 185, 6 How. (Missp) R 386 1 Ves & B. 539, 2 Danul. Ch. P 611, Mitf Eq P 241

The presumption, then, from lapse of time being fully explained in the bill, there can be no objection on this ground on demurrer. As to the Mississippi case on this head, we must remark, that in this respect that Court has been equally unfortunate in the citation of authority. The case of Smith vs Clay was cited as the leading authority. Now the question in that case, (as every lawyer knows) was whether a bill of review could be brought after twenty years, for manifest error apparent on the face of the record, and it was very properly held that it could not, as there was not, and could not be any excuse for the delay. See 2 Sch & Lef 632.

It is true the learned Chancellor in that case recognizes the well established rule in equity, that if a party slumbers upon his rights and acquiesces for a great length of time, he cannot have relief in a Court of Equity.

But it is also a well recognized rule in equity, as is well said by Lord Chancellor Manners in 2 Ball & Beat, 137, that "In order to charge a party with acquiescence, you must affect him with a knowledge of those facts in which he has acquiesced." For the very term acquiescence implies either previous sanction or subsequent ratification 30 Eng L & Eq 150.

In Marker vs. Marker, 9 Hare 16, 41 Eng, Ch R 15. Mr Vice Chancellor Turner says. "Parties cannot, I think, be said to acquiesce in the claims of others, unless they are fully cognizant of their rights to dispute them."

The Court of Appeals of South Carolina, in Shannon vs. White 6 Rich'd Eq R 101, in speaking on this subject holds this strong language "That it would not be sufficient to prove that the Plaintiff had a suspicion of

the fraud   But it is necessary to bring home to the Plaintiff a knowledge of the facts constituting the fraud "

For as Mr. Justice Swift, in Beach vs Catlin, 4 Day's
Conn R 293 well says   "A circumstance to furnish presumptive evidence against a party should be brought home
to his knowledge

In Murray vs Palmer 2 Sch & Lef 486, Lord Redesdale admirably remarks   'Now, I take it that nothing
will amount to a confirmation of a fraudulent transaction
but an act done by the party after he has become *fully*
aware of the fraud that has been practiced '

And Judge Story, in Flaggs vs Mann et al, 2 Sum R
491 451 563, lays down the rule that vague reports and
rumors from strangers and suspicion of notice though a
strong suspicion are not sufficient grounds on which to
charge a party with notice   At page 563, this eminent
jurist says   The doctrine stated at the bar is well founded, that, in order to make such acquiescence binding on
Flagg it should be proved that he had *full knowledge of
all the facts affecting his* legal and equitable rights, etc
And to the same effect are the cases in 4 Dess 474 3
Dess. 239

There is nothing then in the principle of the case of
Smith vs Clay adverse to us or that at all justifies the
Court in Mississippi in its opinion in Buckner & Stanton
vs Calcote   And Judge Goldthwaite in 5 Alab (N S.)
R 108 has well remarked   I think there has sometimes
been a great misapprehension of the celebrated decisions of
Lord Camden in Smith vs Clay Amb 645, but better
reported in Bro C C 639, and of Lord Redesdale, in
Hovenden vs Lord Annesly 2 Sch, & Lef 633   Neither

of those most eminent men intended to be considered as saying that all cases were within the influence of time for the judgment of the first is given with reference to a bill of review, and the case of a concealed deed, is by him expressly excepted, and in the opinion of the last, it is conceded (see page 633), that a trustee *in possession of the trust estate* can never avail himself of the lapse of time as against the *cestui que trust*

Lord Camden then most clearly never intended by his decision in Smith vs Clay, to give any countenance to fraud through lapse of time but on the contrary, he like every other learned and upright judge and author discountenanced every species of fraud

In Bennett vs Colley, 2 M & R 225 7 Cond Eng Ch. 342, it was held that thirty years acquiescence of a party ignorant of his rights was neither a waiver or a confirmation of anything done against him See also Alden vs Gregory, 2 Edan 280

For a party, as Sir William Grant in 2 Meriv 361, well remarks ' Could not be said to acquiesce in acts which he did not know he had a right to dispute

"And so general, indeed, (says Robert's on Fraud Conv 521-2) is the condemnation of all fraudulent acts by the law of England that a fraudulent estate is said, in the masculine language of the books to be no estate in the judgment of the law

' All the partialities of the law expire under its antipathy to fraud

We may well say then in the impressive language of Chief Justice Kent, in Sands vs Codwise, 4 J R 599, ' It would not become a Court of Equity to take a single step to save harmless, a party detected in a fraudulent combination to cheat. No right can be deduced from an act founded in actual fraud

For as Chancellor Kent has well said, 'length of time is no bar to a fraud in equity Marks vs Pell, 1 J. Ch R 594, 598

Lord Brougham also in 3 Eng L & Eq R 24, uses this strong and forcible language "I, too say that no time will run to protect and screen fraud I too say that a Court of Equity will overleap the barrier of time to get at the fraudulent parties and their deeds, and to undo those deeds, and to prevent any one, whether accomplice or innocent, from profiting by the fruits of fraud I, too say that the length of time which has elapsed " (37 and 39 *years,*) "is not a bar to this suit See also Bowen vs Evands, House of Lords Ca 257

And this Court too through Mr Justice Story, in Prevost vs Gratz, 6 Wheat 498, has well and admirably said

And in a case where fraud is imputed and proved, length of time ought not upon principles of eternal justice to be admitted to repel relief'

'On the contrary, it would seem that the length of time during which the fraud had been successfully concealed and practiced, is rather an aggravation of the offence, and calls more loudly on a Court of Equity to grant ample and decisive relief'

IV. The 5th section of the bankrupt act is not a bar to a suit where a party proves his claim and takes a dividend without any knowledge that the discharge was fraudulently obtained

[To be inserted 4 lines from bottom of page 78]

Well may we say then,

'The gorgeous East, with richest hand
Showers on her kings barbaric pearl and gold

in no greater abundance, or more rich profusion, than do
the authorities contribute their golden and inexhaustible
stores in support of the rule that no time will run to screen
and to protect fraud

It is said that the 5th section of the bankrupt act which provides as follows 'And no creditor or other person coming in and proving his debt or other claim shall be allowed to maintain any suit at law or in equity therefore but shall be deemed thereby to have waived all right of action and suit against such bankrupt " is a bar notwithstanding we have positively alleged (and the demurrer admits the truth of the same) that we had no knowledge or information whatever of the frauds when we proved our claims and received a dividend This we think is manifestly erroneous

That this section was never designed or intended to be a bar in cases of *fraud subsequently discovered*, is to our mind clear beyond all doubt There is something so monstrous and revolting to every principle of justice, in the proposition that this section is a bar and a protection to any and every species of fraud perpetrated by the bankrupt notwithstanding the creditor had no knowledge of the same until after he had proved his claim and received a dividend, that we are constrained to believe that Congress never designed so great an enormity

If, therefore by any principle or rule of construction the Court can avoid imputing to Congress such a design as would necessarily be included in such a construction as would make the 5th section a bar in cases of *even* subsequently discovered fraud, we think that construction ought and will be adopted

The whole design, scope, history, and spirit of the act seem to us to repel the idea, that Congress intended by any of its provisions to afford any protection to one who had wilfully (and, that too, under all the sanctity and solemnity of an oath,) violated both the very words and spirit of the statute by committing frauds, not only upon the just rights of creditors but fraud upon the Court and the laws of the land

The voluntary clause of the act was a new principle in bankruptcy, (8 Iredell, (N C) R 142) and many eminent statesmen and judges both before and after the passage of the law, were opposed to this provision and seriously doubted not only the constitutionality of the same, but its policy from the easy and tempting mode it afforded of obtaining a release from one s debts and the frauds consequent thereon   See 2 Kent Com 471, 7th ed n. c , ib 477 n b

It was this branch of the statute ' (says Chancellor Kent, 2 Com 473, n) ' that brought the system and I think justly into general discredit and condemnation, and led to the repeal of the law

But to obviate the objections to the law, there is seen throughout the entire act one grand principle, paramount and supreme over all others and that principle is _good faith and honesty_ on the part of the bankrupt

That great principle was regarded by all as the

' Spiritus untus alit, totamque infusa per artus
Mens agitat molem et magno se corpore miscet '

If then, good faith and honesty on the part of the bankrupt were found wanting, he was not to be allowed his discharge and was moreover subjected to all the pains and penalties of wilful and corrupt perjury   With such guards, shields and checks, as the sanctity of an oath, the pains and penalties of perjury and the refusal of a discharge, if an honest and fair surrender was not made interposed and

designed to secure, protect and extort a fair and honest
surrender on the part of the bankrupt, it would be strange
indeed, if in such an act, thus guarding the rights of creditors, we should find another provision of the same act, not
only countenancing, but absolutely shielding and protecting the fraudulent bankrupt in his iniquity against the
pursuit of his wronged and injured creditors

An act embodying such a principle, and affording such
protection to the fraudulent and perjured bankrupt, would
justly deserve to be classed with that great and stupend-
ous fraud act of Georgia known as the ' Yazoo Fraud
which was so abhorrent to the moral sense and every
principle of justice, that the act was not only pronounced
unconstitutional, fraudulent and void, was not only repealed but it was burnt by the common hangman, in the
presence of the whole assembly and an indignant and out-
raged and injured people, and the record of it expunged
from the statute book and its foul traces effaced from the
land

Can it be, then, that Congress designed this provision in
the 5th section of the bankrupt act as a protection and a
premium for the successful perpetration and concealment
of fraud ?

We must say, we think not notwithstanding its general
language, for it is a rule, of universal recognition, in all
courts and all countries, in the construction of statutes to
construe the same so as to effect as near as possible the
design of the law-makers, as evinced by the *whole act*

In the case of Peck et al vs Jenness et al , 7 How R
622-3, this Court in construing the bankrupt act after
stating that the fourth section provided that the certificate

11

.

when granted, was a discharge of all debts, and that it was contended under this provision that as the debt was discharged no judgment could be rendered, and that consequently the attachment based on the debt must fall with it says This conclusion would be undoubtedly correct, if we construe this section of the act by itself without regard to other provisions of the same act

"But it is among the elementary principles with regard to the construction of statutes that every section, provision, and clause of a statute shall be expounded by a reference to every other and if possible every clause and provision shall avail and have the effect contemplated by the legislature One portion of a statute should not be construed to annul or destroy what has been clearly granted by another The most general and absolute terms of one section, may be qualified and limited by conditions and exceptions contained in another, so that all may stand together

And in the case of Brown vs Duchesne, 19 How R 194, Chief Justice Taney, after stating that the general words in a certain clause of a statute, if taken by themselves and literally construed without regard to the object in view, would seem to sanction the claim of the Plaintiff, well and admirably says But this mode of expounding a statute has never been adopted by any enlightened tribunal, because it is evident that in many cases it would defeat the object which the legislature intended to accomplish And it is well settled that, in interpreting a statute, the Court will not look merely to a particular clause in which general words may be used, but will take in connection with it the whole statute (or statutes on the same subject) and the objects and policy of the law as indicated by its various provisions, and give to it such a construction as will carry into execution the will of the Legislature, as thus ascertained according to its true intent and meaning

Judge Porter also in the case of Cox vs Williams 5 N S 141-2 has well said ' When the terms in which a law is drawn up lead us by a strict interpretation to consequences contrary to common sense, and destructive of private right it is our duty to construe them in such a way as will avoid these consequences The *will* of the legislature is certainly to be obeyed, but the literal meaning of the words used is only one way of ascertaining it It must be sought also in the whole context, in the object of the law, in the evil to be remedied and above all in the conviction sincerely entertained by this Court, that the representatives of the people do not intend to violate first principles '

So in Ardry vs Audry et al 16 La R 268, Judge Martin, too holds this strong and forcible language "That even when a law is clear and unambiguous, the letter may be disregarded with the *honest intention* of seeking its spirit When therefore the letter of the law leads to an absurd conclusion, the Judge is bound to recede from it until he arrives at a reasonable conclusion

And in Buhol vs Boudousque et al 8 N S R. 430 Judge Porter admirably says ' When the terms of a part of a law, taken in their literal sense, lead to absurd and inconvenient results or violate any great principle of natural or social rights, Courts of Justice in all countries have been in the habit of seeking for the intention of the legislature in the scope and object of the whole enactment and if from a view of the whole law, or from other laws in *pari materia*, the evident intention is different from the literal import of the terms employed in a particular part of the law that intention is held to control, because it is really the will of the legislature '

So in Jackson vs Collins 3 Cowen's R 89, 96, the Supreme Court of New York very forcibly remarks ''Whenever the intention of the makers of a statute can be discovered, it ought to be followed with reason and discretion in the construction of the statute, although such construction seem contrary to the letter of the statute Bac Ab tit Stat 1, 15 John 380, per Ch J Thompson

' A thing which is within the letter of the statute is not within the statute unless it be within the intention of the makers This position is fully established and illustrated by the cases cited on the part of the Plaintiff ''

And it is a rule without an exception in the construction of statutes, that they will never be construed in a Court of Equity so as to protect a fraud

' Fraud '' (says this Court, 15 Peters, 594,) ' will vitiate any, even the most solemn transactions and an asserted title to property, founded upon it is utterly void '

However positive may be the language of any statute it cannot be construed so as to protect a party in the perpetration of a fraud In the case of Pratt vs. Northampton et al., 5 Mason R 103-4, Judge Story held that a party who had obtained the settlement of his final account as administrator by fraud, could not claim the protection of the statute, which said that such settlement should be ' final and *conclusive*' unless objected to within a specified time The language of the act as given in the above case is That the settlement of the accounts of any executor administrators or guardian by the Court of Probate or in case of appeal, by the Supreme Court of Probate, shall be *final and conclusive on all parties concerned therein, and shall not be subject to re-examination in any way or manner whatever*

Commenting on this broad comprehensive and unrestricted language, that eminent Jurist says ' This language cannot be considered as giving any higher or stronger efficacy to a probate decree than a judgment possesses at the common law Upon general principles, fraud avoids the latter, and the same doctrine has been uniformly applied to all instruments and proceedings however solemn

The cases of Sims vs Slocum (3 Cranch 307) and Ammiden vs. Smith (1 Wheat R 447,) admit the general principle, and turn upon distinct considerations There is the more reason for applying the doctrine in the present case because the administrator at the time of the settlement, united in himself, also the character of guardian of the Plaintiffs and, as minors they had no means of redress except through him To say, therefore that his own fraud should, under such circumstances bind them, would be to subvert the very foundation of justice '

The principle and reasoning of the above decision would seem to apply with great force to this case It was the duty of the bankrupt to make a fair and honest surrender He called and compelled his creditors to come into Court He stood there as the guardian of their rights under the solemn sanction of an oath, that he had acted fairly and honestly towards all. The creditors knew of no fraud, and had a right to rely, in the absence of information to the contrary upon his own sworn voluntary conduct and duty. Whilst the frauds perpetrated were concealed they had no means of redress except through him. They were powerless to act until the frauds were discovered. Under such circumstances, the 5th section, notwithstanding its general language, cannot be construed to be a bar, without subverting the very foundations of justice itself.

So in Varmeter vs Jones, 2 Green (N. J.) Ch. R. 523-4. Chancellor Vroom holds the same doctrine as laid down by Judge Story that a party who has perpetrated a fraud under a statute can obtain no protection under such statute however general its language. The learned Chancellor after citing numerous authorities to show that judgments awards, verdicts, and decrees might and would be relieved against, by a Court of Equity *for fraud*, says 'And with regard to decrees of the Orphan's Court on the final settlement of accounts although the legislature has declared that the sentences of those Courts *shall be final and conclusive upon all parties*, and exonerate and discharge them from the claims of creditors except in certain specified cases when the accounts may be opened by the Courts themselves, yet it has been decided here, on demurrer that the power and jurisdiction of this Court is not taken away or abridged by that enactment and that the decrees of the Orphan's Courts may be looked into and relieved against on the ground of fraud This is no longer an open question.' See also 15 Ohio R. 666 7. 15 Mass 519

If then a statute which contained a provision equally positive and prohibitory, was not a bar in cases of fraud (as we have seen it was not in both of the above cases) how is it possible to hold the 5th section a bar in cases of even subsequently discovered fraud?

To our mind there is no difference in the principle. If fraud will prevent the bar in one case it must equally do so in the other.

Upon general principles, then, as well as the policy and spirit of the bankrupt act, the 5th section is not and cannot be a bar where the creditor is ignorant of the fraud on the part of the bankrupt, when he proves his claim and takes a dividend.

For the authorities are unanimous in support of the position that a Court of Equity will relieve in cases of mistake as to the facts even though there be no fraud. And the law now seems well settled that a party will also be relieved in cases of mere mistake as to the operation and effect of a law. 27 Eng. L. & Eq. R. 326, 4 Dana's R. 314-318, 3 B. Monroe 510, 11 Ohio R. 223 ib. 480, *American Jurist* for April and July, 1840.

How much more then, should a party be relieved in a case like the present (even if absolutely within the statute) where fraud is coupled with mistake both as to the operation of the law and the facts.

"For," says the Court in 5 Dana's R. 196, "there is no act however solemn, that may not be impeached if vitiated by fraud; and fraud consists in the suppression of truth or the representation of falsehood."

And in the case of Buckingham et al vs McLean 13 How. R. 166 this Court in an elaborate and well considered opinion, as to the proper construction of certain provisions of the bankrupt act well and truly says "The two great objects of the law were to grant a discharge to honest debtors who should conform to its provisions, and to distribute their property ratably among all their creditors '

It is therefore clear that the law makers never designed any provision of the law to protect and shield a *fraudulent* bankrupt. Its provisions of exemption relate to *honest* bankrupts, and not to fraudulent ones

Such being the objects of the act, it should receive (as we have no doubt it will) such a construction, as will be in harmony with, and carry out the great leading objects of the law

Now upon examining the bankrupt act, it will be seen that there are several classes of cases to which the provisions of the 5th section were intended to apply, and which are perfectly consistent with the great leading objects of the legislature in the act, to wit the protection of the rights of creditors against fraudulent bankruptcies and for a *pro rata* distribution of all the bankrupt's effects among *all* his creditors, where it could be done without interfering with rights previously vested The *first* class of cases to which it will apply is that of fiduciary debts, from which the decree in bankruptcy, though obtained *bona fide*, does not discharge the debtor In this case if the creditor would elect to come in and prove his debt, and take a *pro rata* dividend of the bankrupt's effects, he will be held to his election of sharing in the assets surrendered, and will not afterwards be allowed to proceed personally against the bankrupt, if he

obtains a discharge not impeachable for fraud 2 Barb.
Ch R 530, Chapman vs Forsyth, 2 How (S C) R. 202

There is also a *second* class of cases to which the fifth
section applies, viz creditors whose liens are preserved by
the proviso to the *second section* Proof under the fifth
section is a waiver of the lien, as the two rights, a share
of the dividend, and an enforcement of the lien, would
be inconsistent with the provisions of the fifth section —
23 Missp (1 Cush) 75. Briggs vs. Stevens, Law Rep
(Oct No 1844) 281

A *third* class of cases to which it will apply, is that of
foreign creditors, who, though not bound by the discharge
in bankruptcy, would be estopped from claiming against
it, if they accepted the provisions and benefits of the act
and the proceedings under the same 2 Barb Ch R 530,
26 Wend 54 See 7 Met 152, ib 424

Again, proof under the fifth section would suspend the
right of the creditor to proceed in any other Court, while
it was undecided whether a discharge should be granted
or not, for until the discharge or proof before the Commissioner, a creditor was at liberty to pursue his remedies
in any Court 5 Law Rep. 163.

And in case of a second bankruptcy, the party could
not, according to the *twelfth section*, be discharged, unless
his estate produced sufficient to pay every creditor *seventy-
five* cents on the dollar, after paying all charges

This is, then, another unanswerable reason why a party
is not barred from suit in all cases under the fifth section
If a party would be barred in case of discovered fraud he
would, on the same principle be barred if he proved his
claim in a second bankruptcy, though the bankrupt was

12

refused a discharge, in consequence of his estate not paying *seventy-five per cent* to every creditor, as required by the twelfth section

It is, therefore, manifest that the fifth section must be construed with reference to the other provisions, in order to make the act consistent in its different provisions. In all the cases stated above, if the party came in and proved his claim, and received a dividend, he could not say he was not within the law, but like any other creditor who was within the terms of the act, he would be bound by the discharge, unless the same was impeachable for fraud

These views are ably sustained by Chancellor Walworth in a most elaborate and well considered opinion, in the case of Haxtun vs Corse 2 Barb Ch. R 507, where he lays down the rule clearly and unequivocally, that proof before the commissioner will not deprive the party of his right to impeach the discharge for fraud, where he was ignorant of the fraud at the time the proof was made

The learned Chancellor, at pp 529–531 of the above case, says "Indeed if the counsel for the respondents is right in supposing that the proof of a debt, under the proceedings in bankruptcy, is an absolute bar to all claims upon the future acquisitions of the bankrupt, even when the discharge is denied," (but it will be noted, the statute has no exceptions whatever,) ' those who have not proved their debts, are the only class of creditors who have any interest in opposing the bankrupt's discharge For, in that case it must be a matter of entire indifference to those creditors who have proved their debts whether the discharge is or is not granted, as their rights would be precisely the same in either event.

· And it would be absurd to suppose that the framers of
the act had made this provision authorizing the creditors
who had proved their debts specially, and all other persons in interest generally, to come in and oppose the discharge if by another provision of the same statute, the
mere fact of having proved their debts was to deprive
them of all claim upon the person or future acquisitions
of the bankrupt, even if their opposition to the discharge
was successful. 1 conclude, therefore, notwithstanding
the general language contained in the fifth section of the
act—that the creditors who come in and prove their debts,
shall not be allowed to maintain any suit at law or in
equity therefor—the law makers did not intend that the
proving of debts by creditors should be an absolute aban-
donment of all claim against the future acquisitions of
their debtor, if his discharge was refused or if it was void
for any of the frauds specified in the act but merely that
the proving of debts, under the decree, should be considered as a waiver of the rights of the creditors to institute any suits or proceedings at law or in equity, which
were in any way inconsistent with the election of such
creditors to obtain satisfaction of their debts out of the
property of the bankrupt under the decree, and as a consent to be bound by the discharge, in case the bankrupt
should obtain one which was not impeachable for fraud or
wilful concealment of his property

" This rational construction, which I am disposed to put
upon this provision of the statute, would not, however,
deprive creditors who had come in and proved their
debts, but who had successfully resisted the fraudulent
bankrupt's discharge, of all claim to his future acqui-

sitions. Nor would it deprive them of the right which is given under the fourth section of the act to impeach the discharge for fraud or wilful concealment of property in case such fraud should be *discovered after* the discharge had been obtained, where they had not litigated the question of fraud, upon the proceedings in bankruptcy, so as to be estopped by the decision of the Court or jury, from setting up the same matter again.

" But my opinion is founded upon the fact, that to give the construction to the general language of the fifth section of the bankrupt act, which is contended for by the counsel for the respondents, would be to make that provision of the statute wholly inconsistent with the evident intention of the law makers, as evidenced by several other provisions of the same act."

These views of Chancellor Walworth are in exact conformity with the whole design, scope, and policy of the act, and as they comport with natural justice they are such as should commend themselves to the most favorable consideration of the Court. It is true, his Honor, in the above case held that the suit in its then form could not be maintained, as the party by proving had discontinued his suit, and this fact will doubtless be pressed on this Court, as was done in the Mississippi case, for the purpose of weakening the force of his reasoning. But on the contrary, we deem him perfectly consistent, both in his reasoning and in his conclusion. For, undoubtedly, a party by proving would discontinue his suit even if he successfully opposed the discharge of the bankrupt. 2 Barb. Ch. 532. Surely, then, if one was granted, though impeachable for fraud subsequently discovered, the suit must likewise be regarded as discontinued by the proof.

For the object of the statute was to protect a party from suit by a creditor who proved, during the intermediate time between the decree of bankruptcy and the refusal or the granting of a discharge 2 Barb Ch. 530 To effectuate this purpose, therefore, all suits by a creditor who proves must be held discontinued, whether a discharge is refused or one obtained which is impeachable for fraud.

But this in no way would prevent a party from commencing a *new* action

Chancellor Walworth's conclusion, then, in Haxtun vs Corse, is perfectly consistent with his reasoning in relation to the fifth section not being a bar in cases of *subsequently discovered fraud.*

And in the matter of Grant, 5 Law Rep 13, Judge Story holds that a bankrupt may, on the passing of the decree enter into business, and hold property, " subject of course to the contingency of obtaining a discharge, *for if the bankrupt fails to obtain a discharge,* ALL *his property* will at last be subject to the claims of all his creditors '

If the future acquisitions of the bankrupt, then, in the event of his failure to obtain a discharge, will be liable and subject (as Judge Story says it will) to the claims of *all* his creditors, of course the proof of their claims and the receipt of their proportionate share of the fund surrendered, would not be a bar to any further claim For if such would be the effect resulting from the mere proof of their claims and the receipt of their dividends, then the law would impose a penalty on the creditors for taking what this same law gives them the right to take, and would be to discharge the party, notwithstanding the Court under the mandate of the law had refused a discharge to the fraudulent bankrupt

But Judge Story (5 Law Rep 452,) and Judge Betts (5 Law Rep 320) have both *held* that a creditor must prove his debt without any qualifications or reservations before he can be allowed to take any part in the bankrupt proceedings See also 5 Law Rep 225, 228

And yet in 7 Met R 152, the learned Court in Massachusetts, held, that a party who had proved his claim, and who had been permitted to withdraw his proof of the same, might sue the bankrupt

The ground of this decision was, that the party had not enjoyed all the rights of a creditor, (his full share of the property of the bankrupt) as contemplated by the act See 5 Law Rep 228

But, do not these reasons apply with much greater force in favor of a creditor whose rights, under the proceedings, have been defrauded and who was absolutely bound by the proceeding, whether he participated in the same or not ? In the case of a discharge obtained by fraud, he has not enjoyed the rights of a creditor, as contemplated by the act, and is, therefore not barred from suit, upon the discovery of the fraud

And that such is the law, we entertain no earthly doubt

It is true, a case in 31 Me R 192, is relied on as holding a different doctrine But on examination it will be found wholly inapplicable to the case made by the bill, and does not support the opposite doctrine to the extent claimed for it.

That was a case at law, and there is nothing in the case

to show the fraud was discovered after the taking of a dividend

In that case the Court rested its opinion *first* on the ground that a party who proved his claim had a full opportunity in bankruptcy to object to a discharge being granted on the ground of fraud, and, *secondly*, that if he failed or neglected to make the objection that the discharge was *res judicata* and could never afterwards be controverted

From the first ground it would seem but reasonable to suppose the party knew of the fraud, and that the Court in Maine did not regard the mere fact of the proof and the receipt of a dividend as a bar If it did not so consider, why did it say that he had the fullest opportunity to object to a discharge ' If the mere fact of proof would bar, as contended, then it was a matter of entire indifference to the creditor who proved his claim whether the bankrupt obtained a discharge or not

If his debt was absolutely barred by proof he could have no further concern or interest in the matter, and it would then be idle as well as useless, for the Court to afford him an opportunity to oppose and prevent a discharge But the Court in Maine evidently must have considered that a party who proved his claim, and successfully resisted a discharge, would be entitled to sue the bankrupt, else why does it say that he had a right to object, or or that if he neglect or fail to prevent the party obtaining a discharge that the judgment is then, as far as he is concerned, *res judicata* ? If such be not the case, for what purpose does the law and the Court give the party who has proved the fullest opportunity to oppose the discharge ' It does seem that the only object that a party could possibly have in opposing a discharge would be to save his debt from extinguishment For if this be not the case, in the event of successful opposition to a discharge then indeed would opposition to granting a discharge be an idle and useless ceremony on the part of all creditors

It is but natural, then, to suppose from the reasoning of the Court in 31 Me , that it undoubtedly must have considered, that a creditor who had proved and was successful in his opposition to a discharge, had a right to sue and recover the residue of his debt For if it did not so consider, it was wholly unnecessary for the Court to endeavor. by its reasoning, to show that the fullest opportunity had been afforded the party to oppose and prevent the discharge

This case therefore cannot be regarded as sustaining the doctrine that the mere fact of proof is an absolute bar. Nor can it be considered as an authority for a case like the present In this case the frauds were unknown and undiscovered at the time of the discharge But the reasoning of the Court in Maine proceeds on the ground that the party in that case had the fullest opportunity to object, and if he failed or neglected to oppose he had no ground of relief Now this reasoning would apply to one who with full information of the frauds, had failed and neglected to oppose the granting of a discharge. But it is wholly inapplicable to the case made by the bill

For, as was well said in Fermor's case, 3 Co 77, in relation to a fraudulent feoffment, " How could he make his entry or bring his action when he knew not of the feoffment which did the wrong?" So in a case of bankruptcy, how could a party who had no knowledge of fraud be said to have an opportunity, or to neglect to make opposition to a discharge on the ground of fraud?

To so hold "would not savor of reason,' as is well said by the distinguished Chancellor Glenn in 28 Miss R 463 in reviewing the case in Maine and to whose elaborate and well considered opinion we would specially invite the attention of this Court, as a triumphant answer to the opinion of the High Court of Mississippi in the same case See on this point, 28 Miss R 457–465

And in Reynell vs Sprye Sprye vs Reynell, 8 Hare 255, 32 Eng Ch R 255 Vice Chancellor Wigram very admirably says But if parties are ignorant of facts on which their rights depend or erroneously assume that they know those rights, and deal with their property accordingly, not upon the principle of compromising doubts, this Court will relieve against such transactions Stockley vs Stockley, 1 V & B. 23, Harvey vs Coocke, 4 Russ 34 '

It is, therefore, but reasonable and just to suppose the Court in Maine never intended its remarks on the first point to apply to a case of *subsequently discovered fraud*

And as to the last ground on which the cause in Maine is rested, viz, that where a creditor comes in and proves his claim before the discharge is granted, the discharge as to him is *res judicata* and conclusive, we must most respectfully say, that in this the Court was mistaken, as directly the opposite doctrine has been held by the learned Courts in Massachusetts and Tennessee, and these decisions are in exact accordance with the express provision of

13

the bankrupt act which gives the creditor the right to impeach the discharge for fraud

In Beckman vs Wilson 9 Met. R 438 Mr Justice Dewey in speaking on the subject of a discharge being *res judicata*, where the creditors had unsuccessfully opposed the same says ' As to the first of these objections it seems to us that the proceedings by the creditors under the provisions of the second section of that act, which authorizes them to interpose objections to the granting of the discharge and the issuing of the certificate *are in no respect a bar to setting up fraud in avoidance of the discharge under the authority given by the fourth section* Both modes of proceeding are authorized by the statute, and the creditors may avail themselves of one, *or of both as they may deem expedient.* The purposes of the bankrupt law is answered, so far as it looks to the case of the debtor, if honest debtors, acting in accordance with the principles of fair dealing and the equal distribution of their assets among all their creditors, are secured in the full enjoyment of the benefits of a discharge. As to *such debtors, these objections, whether interposed before or after granting their discharge, will be wholly unavailing* As to *fraudulent debtors*, and those who would designedly violate the *great principles* of the bankrupt code the statute may properly be *liberally construed* in favor of creditors and to defeat unjust preferences In the opinion of the Court, the statute fully warrants the Plaintiff in taking these objections in avoidance of the discharge in bankruptcy notwithstanding other creditors may have *relied upon the same acts* as a ground of opposition to the granting of such discharge originally

And in the case of Gupton vs Connor 11 Humphreys R 287, 289 291, Mr Justice Totten in speaking on this same subject, says · As a general proposition it is certainly true. that the judgment of a Court of competent jurisdiction, remaining in force, is conclusive as to parties and privies upon the matter adjudicated We do not think however, that this principle has any application to the present case It must turn upon a just construction of the statute in question When the statute introduced and established the principle of voluntary bankruptcy for the benefit of the debtor, it became very material to guard and protect the rights of the creditor against its abuse and it therefore established another principle and that is that a fraudulent bankruptcy shall be of no avail for the debtor against his creditor If the fraud appear pending his suit against his creditors no decree of discharge could be made , if it appear afterwards, its effect is to annul and avoid the discharge and certificate as though they had never been obtained The proceedings in the bankrupt court is in effect the suit of the debtor against his creditors and it contemplates a full and fair surrender of all his property and effects for their benefit and a discharge of the debtor from all his liabilities to them He is entitled to his discharge only upon the condition that all his property and effects have been fully and fairly surrendered If he obtain it without complying with this condition, it was a fraud upon the law, and upon his creditors, and the circumstance that the creditors dissented from it and contested it, does not legalize and perfect the fraudulent transaction, and make it effectual and conclusive against them The certificate is *prima facie* conclusive as to the validity of the discharge, subject, however, to be impeached for fraud, if any were perpetrated in obtaining it It may be impeached by any of the creditors against whom it shall be plead, whether they contested his discharge or not. The right depends upon the legal effect given to the certificate It is not absolutely conclusive as to any of the creditors but may be impeached, and it has no greater or less effect against one creditor than another. It was in the contemplation of the legislative mind at the time this law was made, that it might be, as it no doubt may be perverted and abused, and become a fruitful source of fraud and imposition upon the rights of creditors

"To check and guard against this tendency, it adopts in effect the principle before alluded to, that the bankrupt's certificate, though formally obtained, shall be of no avail to him if it were fraudulently obtained So that, if the fact of fraud appear at any time, it may be replied and relied upon as an answer to the plea of the certificate and this principle applies in favor of all the creditors alike and in common, without regard to the circumstance that some of them had contested and others acquiesced in the bankrupt's discharge

These able, just and unanswerable views and the reasoning of the learned Courts in Massachusetts and Tennessee, (with the numerous cases cited above under the head of equity jurisdiction, and fully sustaining the position that a judgment obtained by fraud is void and may be so declared in any Court whenever the fraud is shown,) must be quite conclusive against the opposite principle in 31 Maine

For not only is the whole current of authority against it, but reason as well as the entire policy and design of the bankrupt act require, that a fraudulent discharge should be wholly unavailing to the fraudulent bankrupt

So protean, indeed, are the forms, and so chameleon the hues, which fraud assumes, that it is a clearly recognized principle in equity that a party to a suit is never presumed to know or to be able to prevent the successful perpetration and concealment of fraud in obtaining a judgment so as to be concluded or bound by the same 2 Green's (Iowa) R 75.

There is, however, one case in 28 Missp. R 432, in which the decision in 31 Maine was regarded as authority, for the position that a creditor who proves his claim and receives a dividend, without any knowledge of the fraud in obtaining the discharge, is nevertheless barred from ever afterwards suing the bankrupt But as we have shown that the case in Maine does not, in the first place, sustain this doctrine, and is not applicable to the case made by the bill, and in the *second* place that both reason and the entire current of authority are against it, the Mississippi case cannot be regarded as any additional authority It is true this case also cites Chapman vs Forsyth, 2 How as authority, but we think it very clear that it never was intended by this Court to lay down any such doctrine

For in that case this question was not at all involved or considered And the Court, moreover in speaking of the bankrupt and his discharge says ' If, for instance, he owe a debt as executor, and he state it on his schedule as an ordinary one he commits a fraud on the law and the discharge cannot avail him '

It is, therefore manifest the Court in the above case only intended their subsequent remark, ' can never controvert the discharge ' to mean that a fiduciary creditor who not only proved his claim but took his dividend was estopped from saying that it was not within the law, and that he was therefore bound by the discharge in all respects, *unless* he could show that it was fraudulently obtained For it expressly says, if a party ' *commits a fraud on the law, the discharge cannot avail him*

And to avert so great an injustice as it would be to make the proof of a claim and the receipt of a dividend without any knowledge of the fraud, a bar to all further claim against the bankrupt ' does certainly require that the utmost meaning and effect fairly attributable, to them,' (the different provisions of the act) 'should be laid hold of to prevent so great a mischief ' 13 How R 166

For the creditors ' says the Court of Appeals in New York, 4 Seld R 266, were not the less objects of regard of the bankrupt act than the debtor '

The Court in Mississippi, in its construction of the act makes the fifth section a limitation on the general right given under the fourth section to all creditors to impeach the discharge for fraud, and says that the provisions of the fifth section would be useless unless it is so construed In reply to this it might be sufficient for us to say in the language of Mr Justice Swift in Beach vs. Catlin 4 Day s (Conn) R 293, that. 'It would be a new idea to construe a statute liberally for the protection of fraud.'

And would it not be better for it to be a useless provision rather than construed by the Courts as a shield and a protection to any and every species of fraud ' "Courts are to construe an act ' (says the Court in New York) not so liberally as to work injustice but so liberally as to prevent the mischief, and advance the remedy " Jackson vs West, 10 J R 466

But it is an unwarrantable assumption on the part of the Mississippi Court that the provisions of the fifth section must be regarded as a limitation on the right given to all creditors in the fourth section to impeach the discharge for fraud and that it would be useless if this construction is not adopted

Now the fifth section as we have shown above would protect the bankrupt from all suits against him by creditors, who had come in and proved their claims, during the intermediate period of proving and the granting or refusing a discharge See 2 Barb Ch R 530

Here, then we see that the fifth section, in this view of the case, could have full and complete operation and serve a good purpose by protecting the bankrupt from the harassment of suits until it could be decided whether or not he should be discharged This it seems to us, was one of the great purposes for which this section was intended And viewed in this light it is a wise and salutary provision But to hold it a bar and protection for any and every species of fraud, whether a discharge is refused (for the principle goes that length) or one is obtained by fraud, is contrary to every principle of justice and subversive of the whole policy of the bankrupt act *Now would it not be more rational to consider the general right given to all creditors in the fourth section to impeach the discharge for fraud, a limitation to the general language of the fifth section, than to consider the latter section a limitation on the former so as to protect and sanctify fraud?*

If we adopt the former as the rule of construction, then we construe the statute so as to protect the creditor (who is bound by the discharge *if bona fide* obtained, whether he comes in or stays out,) against the fraud of the bankrupt and at the same time preserve the policy and spirit of the law, which only intended and justifies the discharge of *honest* and *not fraudulent* bankrupts How, then was it possible for any Court to so construe the act of Congress as to counteract the whole policy of the law, by making it a protection for the very frauds which it denounces and condemns and against which it so cautiously guarded?

It is true, however that the Court in Mississippi also cites some two or three cases in 5 Law Rep for the doctrine that it is only those who do not prove that are entitled to sue the bankrupt

But in none of these cases was the question, as to the effect of the fifth section in case of the proof of a claim and the receipts of a dividend without any knowledge of fraud, at all involved or considered. See 2 Barb. Ch R 531 They can hardly then be regarded as authority, for the Mississippi Court's position that it is only those who do not prove that are entitled even in cases of subsequently discovered fraud, to contest the discharge of the bankrupt None of those judges, certainly, ever intended their remarks to be construed into a recognition of such a doctrine

On the contrary, Judge Story, in 5 Law Rep 69, asserts that ' The whole policy of the bankrupt act is an equal distribution of the assets among all the creditors.'

So Judge Sprague considers a bankrupt as "divested of all his property for the benefit of all his creditors" by the passing of the decree of bankruptcy 5 Law Rep 24–5   See also 5 Law Rep. 324, ib 306.

And Mr Justice Wayne in delivering the well considered opinion of this Court in Booth vs Clark 17 How R 335, uses this conclusive language "An assignee in bankruptcy is an officer made by the statute of bankruptcy, for the collection of the bankrupt's estate for an equal distribution of it among all of his creditors "

As the whole design and policy of the law then was an equal distribution of the property of the bankrupt among *all* of his creditors, it would be unreasonable to suppose the law makers only intended that those who did not come in and take their proportionate share of the fund surrendered, should have the right to impeach the discharge for fraud

For if the policy of the law, (which was an equal distribution of the property surrendered among *all* the creditors) was carried out, and each creditor took his dividend according to the contemplation of the act, then there would be no one, according to the Mississippi case, who could impeach the discharge, and consequently the general right given in the fourth section to all creditors to impeach the discharge for fraud would be inoperative and useless. A construction, therefore, that would result so injuriously to creditors and so beneficially to fraudulent bankrupts, cannot be a sound or a wise construction

This is still further manifest from the fact that all the property of the bankrupt is divested out of the bankrupt (as we have seen) on the passing of the decree of bank-

14

ruptcy, and vested in an assignee as soon as one is appointed, for the common benefit of *all* the creditors

And Judge Story, in Cheney 5 Law Rep 22-3, expressly holds, that the property so divested is distributable among the creditors whether a discharge is granted or refused

Such being the law, it is very evident that if a discharge is refused, and the assets surrendered are distributed as the law contemplates, among *all* the creditors *pro rata*, that they would still have the right to sue the bankrupt for the residue, otherwise it would have been useless for the Court to refuse the discharge

As the policy of the law then, was both to distribute the property of the bankrupt equally among *all* the creditors, and at the same time to refuse a discharge to a fraudulent bankrupt, it is very obvious that the mere fact of the proof of a claim and the receipt of a dividend will not bar the creditor of the right to sue the bankrupt in case a discharge is refused.

And to illustrate, let us suppose A is declared a bankrupt and that B is his only creditor, and that the property surrendered is not sufficient to pay the debt, and that A's discharge is refused on the opposition of B, his only creditor Now B, in such case according to Judge Story's opinion, is clearly entitled to the property surrendered, and as A's discharge was refused B must have the right to recover the residue, or else A would in fact be discharged from all his debts notwithstanding the Court refused to discharge him on account of fraud It is, therefore, very evident that a creditor who proves and takes a dividend, cannot be barred of suit against the bankrupt if his discharge is refused and yet he is within the very words of the law

It would, therefore, seem too clear to admit of doubt or controversy, that the position that it is only those creditors who do not prove that can sue the bankrupt is not a just or proper construction of the act

And if this be true, as it most undoubtedly is in a case where the discharge is refused, it must, in principle be equally true where the discharge is granted, but is impeachable for fraud

To test and prove the correctness of this, let it be supposed that A (after having made payments and preferences in contemplation of bankruptcy) applies for a discharge and that he owes B, his only creditor $100,000, and that his inventory shows assets to the amount of $10,000, and that B, having no knowledge of any fraud, is unable to make any opposition to A obtaining a discharge, which he of course receives Now, as the property surrendered would be vested in the assignee for B, and no one else, is it not evident that he would be entitled to prove his claim and take the property surrendered, without barring himself of the right of ever after suing the bankrupt in case he discovered the discharge was fraudulently obtained ? If such be not the case, then, B could not take what the law says he shall take, and what no one else can take without, at the same time for ever barring himself from the right to impeach A's discharge for fraud subsequently discovered, and A's fraudulent discharge, thereby, would be a complete protection to him, notwithstanding the act of Congress says it may be impeached for fraud

But it may be said that B, if he wished to save his

right to impeach the discharge, ought not to have proved his claim and received his dividend.

The successful answer to this is, that the property was divested out of A by the decree of bankruptcy and vested absolutely and irrevocably in the assignee for his benefit, and which the law gives him the right to receive and which no one else can take   If he does not take what the law gives to him alone, to whom is it to go?   The answer is, to no one, as there is no other creditor, and the bankrupt by law cannot take until all of the creditors are paid. It is, therefore, *very clear*, that the creditor does not bar himself from suing the bankrupt in cases of fraud subsequently discovered, by the mere fact of proving his claim and taking a dividend

And that the fifth section was only designed as a protection to the bankrupt from the harassment of suits during the intermediate time between the decree of bankruptcy and the granting or refusing a discharge (and not as a shield and a protection to fraud), is further evinced from the fact that it is the discharge and certificate, if *bona fide* obtained that is made a bar   Now if a party obtains his discharge honestly and fairly, the certificate is a complete bar and a protection against all debts provable under the act

From this it results, that the fifth section is no protection to a bankrupt after he has fairly obtained his discharge.   His protection is found in his certificate alone , and this is his complete and impenetrable shield

It is, therefore, seen that the bar of the fifth section would be of no benefit to honest bankrupts after their discharge   And the only effect it can possibly have by hold-

[To be inserted on page 109, end of 8th line]

And in confirmation of which, we would invite the attention of your honors to a case in one of the Western States. And though it be the decision of a court in a State in which, but as yesterday the curtains of the wilderness were rolled back and her smiling plains opened up to the sunlight of civilization and intelligence yet, it is such a decision as must elicit the admiration of every true lover of justice and the law   For it rests upon principles as firm and as solid as the foundations of the everlasting hills And this decision, may t please your Honors, is to be found in 2 Green's (Iowa) R 74–5

In this case, Chief Justice Williams held that a party could not be presumed to be able to prevent fraud, and that a statute which provided that a judgment in partition should be binding and conclusive upon all the parties to the same, only applied to *bona fide* proceedings, and that "it never was intended to cover up proceedings *mala fide*"

Such the language — such the noble sentiments of the court in Iowa   Take the principle of this decision if you will, and subject it to the severest tests   Cast it into the seven-fold heated furnace of scrutiny and investigation, yet like the sons of God of old, it will live amid the flames, and come forth unscathed and unharmed from the fiery ordeal, and like the angel on Minoah's sacrifice, it will mount aloft and soar away to Heaven and sing This principle, then, may it please your Honors, must be quite conclusive against the opposite doctrine of the Mississippi case, which makes the fifth section of the bankrupt act, a bar and a protection to any and every species of fraud upon the part of the bankrupt

ing it a bar against all who prove, will be to make it a
shield and a protection to fraudulent bankrupts, and thus
subvert the whole policy of the law which gives all the
creditors in common the right to impeach the discharge
for fraud, and which only intended that honest bankrupts
should be discharged from their liabilities

On no just principle of construction, then can the Mississippi case be sustained or regarded as authority

And, indeed, the Mississippi Court in order to shelter
and protect itself from the absurd consequences of the
construction it was putting on the act of Congress, was
forced to resort to the spirit and policy of the statute
For in answer to the objection that if the Court construed
the fifth section an absolute bar, that it would conclude a
creditor who had merely proved his claim for the purpose
of opposing a discharge, even if his opposition was successful, it is said by that Court that "this objection is not
sustained by the spirit of the fifth section nor by the general policy of the act," and that the policy of the act and
the true intent of the provision had reference to all creditors coming in and proving their debts in order to be entitled to share in the bankrupt's property, and who should
receive their dividends   But the bar of the fifth section
says nothing about a dividend or a sharing in the property of the bankrupt.   A creditor who comes in and successfully opposes a discharge is as much within the words of
the act as one who takes a dividend, without a knowledge
of the fraud.   How, then, can the Court exempt the former
and not the latter '

If the spirit and policy of the act must be invoked in
the one case to do substantial justice why not invoke that

same spirit to do justice in cases of fraud subsequently discovered? Is there not the same necessity in the one case as in the other to consult the spirit of the act?

To our mind, there is the same necessity, in order to do substantial justice and prevent the party from profiting by his own fraud

Nor will the reference to the sharing in the property of the bankrupt obviate that necessity The statute says ' That *all creditors* coming in and proving their debts, etc *shall be entitled to share in the bankrupt's property and effects pro rata* Now if the creditors successfully oppose the discharge are they not according to this provision entitled to share equally the property of the bankrupt? Most undoubtedly they are For as we have shown above Judge Story (5 Law Rep 19) holds that the property is distributable even if the discharge is refused

In such case, then, is it not a self-evident proposition that the creditors would not be barred by taking that which the law expressly gives them the right to receive? For unless they take their dividends the property could never be distributed and this much of the estate of the bankrupt which has been surrendered for their benefit would be placed forever beyond their reach

The reference, then, to the sharing of the property of the bankrupt will not sustain or justify the Court in its construction of the fifth section

And if the principle fails in a case, as we think we have shown it does, where the discharge is successfully opposed and refused ought it not also on every principle of justice, to be held to fail in a case like the present of subsequently discovered fraud?

If such be not the law then the general creditor, (who is absolutely bound by the discharge, if honestly obtained whether he comes in or stays out) must either prove his claim and take his dividend, and be forever barred of all further claim against the bankrupt or he must forego all benefit and participation in the bankrupt proceedings, lest he bar himself of his right to impeach the discharge, in case he should by possibility discover that it was fraudulently obtained

Would this be reasonable—would it be fair—would it be just towards the creditor? and we may add, is it possible to suppose that Congress designed so great an enormity as the protection of a fraudulent bankrupt, when the creditor had only taken, on compulsion, as it were, what was really and honestly his due? Surely, surely not!

For in Crocker et al vs Stone et al 7 Cushing's Rep 341, it was held by the Supreme Court of Massachusetts, that no discharge in insolvency was valid even as against a creditor who proves his claim, and is himself the assignee, unless the discharge is obtained in strict conformity to law See, also, 4 Cush 529

The English cases, if any should be cited are inapplicable, as their system related to *involuntary* but ours to *voluntary* bankruptcy. 2 Story's R 356, 3 McLean's R 631

And the same is true of our former bankrupt act, and the constructions given to it by the State Courts 3 McLean's R 631

It is, therefore, unnecessary to consider what has been the practice in the English Courts, and the State Courts under the old bankrupt act

It may not, however, be unimportant to refer to a late case in this country, in order to show that no return of a dividend is necessary, but more especially to confirm the principle that a fraudulent discharge will be unavailing The Supreme Court of New Hampshire, in the case of Pierce vs Wood, 3 Foster s R 520, 534, in speaking on this subject, uses this striking and forcible language ' Fraud being established, the compromise became void and the Plaintiff's entire debt would at once be revived, and a clear right of action exist in his favor. And it appears to us that it would be a singular doctrine to hold that before an action can be maintained to recover the balance, that portion of the Plaintiff's demands which had been paid, must first be refunded—that before he can institute a suit for the amount out of which he has been defrauded, he must first repay that which was honestly his due, and which, so far as he was concerned, he has honestly received

" Such a rule would be offering a premium for fraud, and in most cases of the kind, a Plaintiff might better retain the per cent. which he has received, than relinquish that for the uncertainty of recovering the whole " See also 2 Mumf R 69

And the remarks of Mr Roberts, in his commentaries on the Statutes of 13 and 27 Eliz. (Robt Fraud Conv 521-2) would also apply with great force to this case He says

So general, indeed, is the condemnation of all fraudulent acts by the laws of England, that a fraudulent estate is said in the masculine language of the books to be no estate in the judgment of the law It forfeits the protection of every statute which gives confirmation to doubtful titles, and while a disseizer has the benefit of the statutes of fines and limitations in support of his wrongful title a title acquired by covin is indefinitely open to be disputed and even acts, as well *judicial* as other, which of themselves are just and lawful, if infected with fraud, are in judgment of law vicious and unavailing, for the maxim is *quod alias et justum est, si per fraudem petatur, malum et injustum afficitur* All the partialities of the law expire under its antipathy to fraud "

For statutes made in suppression of fraud and deceit bind even the king, (Magdalen College, 11 Rep. 73,) and are to be *beneficially* expounded Booth's case, 5 Rep 77 a.

And in Wimbish vs Tailboys, 1 Plowd Conn 59, it is laid down that statutes made in suppression of fraud and covin shall be equitably expounded even though they are greatly penal See 1 Rep 131.

In Smith vs. Smith, 1 McMull Eq R 135, Chancellor Duncan well says "The statute of frauds says that no action or suit shall be maintained on an agreement relating to lands, which is not in writing, signed by the party to be charged with it, and yet the Court is in the daily habit of relieving, where the party, seeking relief, has been put into a situation which makes it *against conscience* in the other party to insist on the want of writing so signed, as a bar to his relief.

"Courts of Equity decide on equitable grounds, in contradiction to the positive enactment of the statute of frauds though their proceedings are, in words, included in it

"One acknowledged principle on which Courts of Equity

15

give relief, is to prevent an advantage gained by law, from being used against conscience.'

And in 2 Danl. Ch. Pr. 751, the learned author states the rule as follows · "That the Court will not allow a party to avail himself of the statute of frauds for the purpose of committing a fraud

"For " (as Judge Story 2 St Eq sect 768, very admirably and justly says,) " otherwise the statute designed to suppress fraud, would be the greatest protection to it.'

So in this case, if the fifth section be held a bar, then indeed will the statute which was designed to suppress fraud and deceit, (by *giving all the creditors the right to impeach the same for fraud*) become a shield and a protection to those frauds against which the framers of the act have so cautiously and sedulously guarded

And, besides " it would not be very pleasant to stand by and witness the fraudulent conduct of persons in the predicament' of a fraudulent bankrupt, crowned with success Per Hosmer, J 3 Conn. R 284 For a fraudulent transaction or proceeding, as is happily said by Mr Justice Woodbury in 6 How R 120, " cannot receive the countenance of this Court '

And in the case of The State vs Bethune, 8 Iredell's (N. C) R. 142-4, Chief Justice Ruffin well and admirably says "Though it may be in the power of Congress to discharge insolvents from their debts at their own instance it was, we believe, a new principle in the law of bankruptcy, and so strongly tends to encourage men dishonestly to contract debts which they do not intend or mean to pay. as to make it highly proper, as far as possible, to guard the Courts from imposition. and to protect creditors

[To be inserted 2 lines from bottom of page 113]

We have thus, may it please your Honors, referred only to a few of the more prominent of the authorities, to show that on no just and fair principle of construction whatever, can the fifth section of the bankrupt act be held a bar, where the creditor proves his claim and takes a dividend without any knowledge of the fraud of the bankrupt   But did time and circumstances permit, or occasion require, we could refer you to many more   Indeed, may it please your Honors we might go on, like the fair Sultana in the oriental legends for a thousand and one nights, without exhausting the great storehouse of the law   And e'en as in those charming and Eastern stories, so in the authorities, you would behold glowing upon every page, and sparkling in every line, the bright gems and ingots of the law, which illustrate, which beautify, and which adorn the doctrine, that a party who perpetrates a fraud under a statute, will never be allowed in a court of equity, to invoke any provision of that statute to shield and protect him in his fraud from fraud in obtaining discharges. It is enough to put it in the power of a man, after running in debt to spend all his property, and then on his own motion, and upon his own oath, free himself and his future acquisitions from liability to his own creditors

' It is a just and fitting requital to one who attempts to get a discharge by denying that he owns property when in fact he does or by purposely concealing any part of what he does own, to refuse him, in the first place the discharge on any terms and in the next place to hold a discharge, obtained by such means ineffectual and void whenever the fraud shall appear For the Legislature was aware that such dishonest practices might escape the vigilance of the most cautious judge, and intended if they should, that notwithstanding the success in his application the dishonest party should not permanently have the immunities meant for honest insolvents See also, 8 Alab R (N S) 848 864 Sims vs Slocum 3 Cranch 306-7 3 Dess 269-70, 11 Humph R 289 9 Geo 9-14, 15 Alab R 553-4 and foregoing authorities on this subject

We may well say then in the impressive language of the Supreme Court of Massachusetts, in 9 Met R 438 " As to fraudulent bankrupts, and those who would designedly violate the great principles of the bankrupt code the statute may properly be liberally construed in favor of creditors and to defeat unjust preferences "

For a statute made in suppression of fraud has always received the most liberal construction 20 Conn R 394 3 Conn R 29-30. ib. 283-4

The proving of a claim in bankruptcy, therefore where the party has no knowledge of the fraud of the bankrupt can only be considered (as Chancellor Walworth says in his admirable and well considered opinion, in Haxtun vs Corse, 2 Barb. Ch R 529-31,) "as a consent to be bound by the discharge in case the bankrupt should obtain one which was not impeachable for fraud or wilful concealment of his property" "Any other construction," says this learned Chancellor, "would be to make that provision of the statute *wholly inconsistent* with the *evident intention* of the law makers, *as evinced by several other provisions of the same act*"

On every principle, then of reason justice, and the weight of authority, we are firmly convinced and constrained to say that the fifth section is not, and was not designed by Congress as a bar and a protection to the fraudulent bankrupt in cases of *subsequently discovered fraud*

To hold otherwise would be subversive of the great fundamental principles of justice, and make all the provisions of the Act of Congress for the benefit and protection of creditors against the frauds of the bankrupt as unsubstantial and illusory as

> " Dead Sea fruits that tempt the eye
> But turn to ashes on the lips "

L. MADISON DAY
Compl Sol

Lightning Source UK Ltd.
Milton Keynes UK
UKHW030632250722
406332UK00007B/730